AF766371

Human Rights Law and Corporate Regulation

This book argues for an intensely humanist engagement with the company and presents a model of company regulation that is compatible with the protection, respect for and fulfilment of human rights.

Dr Barrett provides a theoretical framing for corporate regulation in the context of human rights States. He argues that States which have ratified the fundamental human rights instruments should, on principle, exclude bodies corporate from the human rights ecosystem, except to the degree necessary to respect property rights of humans and human rights in business. He therefore develops a 'neo-concession' account of the corporation as the basis for a model of corporate regulation to protect human rights. The book outlines and recommends the principal features of a company under a neo-concession model, and the role of regulators in furthering the State's human right obligations. It also delves into the potential issues of technological developments, including decentralised autonomous organisations, and the lessons policymakers can gain from First Nations' approaches to business.

This is a thought-provoking volume that will appeal to scholars in the disciplines of human rights law and corporate governance, as well as policymakers and regulators interested in regulating business for greater societal good.

Jonathan Barrett is an Associate Professor in the School of Accounting and Commercial Law, Victoria University of Wellington Te Herenga Waka, New Zealand. He teaches company law and taxation and researches the practical application of human rights.

Routledge Research in Human Rights Law

Housing, Land and Property Rights
Residential Justice, Conflict Zones and Climate Change
Scott Leckie

The European Convention on Human Rights and the COVID-19 Pandemic
Ronagh J.A. McQuigg

International Human Rights and Local Courts
Human Rights Interpretation in Indonesia
Edited by Aksel Tømte and Eko Riyadi

Defamation and the Right to Freedom of Speech
The UK in Comparative Perspective
Mariette Jones

Bulk Surveillance, Democracy and Human Rights Law in Europe
A Comparative Perspective
Marcin Rojszczak

Surveillance Law, Data Retention and Human Rights
A Risk to Democracy
Matthew White

Domestic Abuse and the European Court of Human Rights
Ronagh J.A. McQuigg

Human Rights Law and Corporate Regulation
A Neo-Concession Approach
Jonathan Barrett

For more information about this series, please visit: www.routledge.com/Routledge-Research-in-Human-Rights-Law/book-series/HUMRIGHTSLAW

Human Rights Law and Corporate Regulation

A Neo-Concession Approach

Jonathan Barrett

Routledge
Taylor & Francis Group
LONDON AND NEW YORK

First published 2025
by Routledge
4 Park Square, Milton Park, Abingdon, Oxon OX14 4RN

and by Routledge
605 Third Avenue, New York, NY 10158

Routledge is an imprint of the Taylor & Francis Group, an informa business

© 2025 Jonathan Barrett

The right of Jonathan Barrett to be identified as author of this work has been asserted in accordance with sections 77 and 78 of the Copyright, Designs and Patents Act 1988.

All rights reserved. No part of this book may be reprinted or reproduced or utilised in any form or by any electronic, mechanical, or other means, now known or hereafter invented, including photocopying and recording, or in any information storage or retrieval system, without permission in writing from the publishers.

Trademark notice: Product or corporate names may be trademarks or registered trademarks, and are used only for identification and explanation without intent to infringe.

British Library Cataloguing-in-Publication Data
A catalogue record for this book is available from the British Library

Library of Congress Cataloging-in-Publication Data
Names: Barrett, Jonathan, 1962- author.
Title: Human rights law and corporate regulation: A Neo-Concession Approach / Jonathan Barrett.
Description: Abingdon, Oxon [UK]; New York, NY: Routledge, 2024. |
Series: Routledge research in human rights law |
Includes bibliographical references and index.
Identifiers: LCCN 2024036973 | ISBN 9781032833781 (hardback) |
ISBN 9781032833835 (paperback) | ISBN 9781003509066 (ebook)
Subjects: LCSH: Social responsibility of business–Law and legislation. |
International business enterprises–Law and legislation. |
Corporation law. | Human rights–Economic aspects. | Concessions.
Classification: LCC K1327 .B37 2024 | DDC 346/.066–dc23/eng/20240813
LC record available at https://lccn.loc.gov/2024036973

ISBN: 9781032833781 (hbk)
ISBN: 9781032833835 (pbk)
ISBN: 9781003509066 (ebk)

DOI: 10.4324/ 9781003509066

Typeset in Times New Roman
by Deanta Global Publishing Services, Chennai, India

For Barina

Contents

1 Introduction

> It is not necessary to agree on a precise theory of the corporation to agree that corporations differ from natural persons in fundamental ways and that a legislature might therefore need to regulate them differently if it is human welfare that is the object of its concern.
>
> … corporations have no consciences, no beliefs, no feelings, no thoughts, no desires. Corporations help structure and facilitate the activities of human beings, to be sure, and their 'personhood' often serves as a useful legal fiction. But they are not themselves members of 'We the People' by whom and for whom our Constitution was established.[1]

These comments made by a Supreme Court Justice relate to a particular US statute, but the themes raised are universal and perennial. Corporations are not 'persons' in the way that human beings are, and they must be regulated to promote human welfare. Furthermore, despite corporations being useful instruments for achieving human objectives, to the extent possible, they should be excluded from consideration of human rights. These are some of the key themes of this study, which focuses on the UK-heritage system of company regulation practised in Australia, Canada and New Zealand. The position of minority Indigenous Peoples is a specific concern of this study,[2] and so these

1 See *Citizens United v Federal Election Commission* 558 US 310, per Justice Stevens (partly concurring) 76.

2 Unless directly citing a text, this study avoids archaic identifiers, such as 'Indian' or 'Aborigine'. The term 'Indigenous Peoples' is mostly used. While all First Nations are Indigenous Peoples, not all Indigenous Peoples are First Nations. In Canada, along with First Nations, Inuit and Métis are identified as Indigenous Peoples. Indigenous communities should, of course, determine their own self-identifiers and these should be respected by outsiders.

I do not have Indigenous genealogy and do not claim to speak for or directly interpret any aspect of Indigenous culture. I recognise that outsider research which comments on Indigenous worldviews and practices may perpetuate colonialism and exercise control over Indigenous culture: see, generally, Linda Tuhiwai Smith, *Decolonizing Methodologies: Research and Indigenous Peoples* (2nd ed, Zed Books, 2012). In conducting this study, I have sought to comply with Te Tiriti o Waitangi Statute of the Victoria University of Wellington Te Herenga Waka.

DOI: 10.4324/9781003509066-1

settler majoritarian states are of particular interest. Ireland, South Africa[3] and the United Kingdom are also relevant. Since all these jurisdictions have ratified the three fundamental human rights instruments,[4] collectively known as the *International Bill of Human Rights* (IBHR),[5] they may be characterised as 'human rights States'. The IBHR instruments are the Universal Declaration of Human Rights (UDHR),[6] the *International Covenant on Economic, Social and Cultural Rights* (ICESCR)[7] and the *International Covenant on Civil and Political Rights* (ICCPR).[8] Despite early resistance,[9] Australia, Canada and New Zealand have also ratified the *United Nations Declaration on the Rights of Indigenous Peoples* (UNDRIP),[10] which has particular relevance to these countries because their settler populations vastly outnumber their Indigenous Peoples.[11] Hong Kong SAR and Singapore may be relevant from a corporate

3 The South African common law is usually characterised as a Roman-Dutch hybrid, but its company law has traditionally followed the British lead. See eg, HS Cilliers et al., *Corporate Law* (2nd ed, Butterworths, 1992) 14.

4 Unlike Conventions and Covenants, UN Declarations are not binding treaties under public international law. In addition to the two covenants, the other five major UN treaties are the UN General Assembly, *Convention Against Torture and Other Cruel, Inhuman or Degrading Treatment or Punishment*, UNTS vol 1465, p 85, 10 December 1984; UN General Assembly, *Convention on the Rights of the Child*, UNTS, vol 1577, p 3, 20 November 1989; UN General Assembly, *International Convention on the Elimination of All Forms of Racial Discrimination*, UNTS, vol 660, p 195, 21 December 1965; UN General Assembly, *Convention on the Elimination of All Forms of Discrimination Against Women*, UNTS, vol 1249, p 13, 18 December 1979; UN General Assembly, *Convention on the Rights of Persons with Disabilities*: resolution/adopted by the General Assembly, A/RES/61/106, 24 January 2007.

5 See 'Fact Sheet No.2 (Rev.1), The International Bill of Human Rights', *OHCHR* (Report, 1996) <https://www.ohchr.org/Documents/Publications/FactSheet2Rev.1en.pdf>.

6 *Universal Declaration of Human Rights*, GA Res 217A (III), UN GAOR, UN Doc A/810 (10 December 1948) (UDHR).

7 UN General Assembly, *International Covenant on Economic, Social and Cultural Rights*, UNTS, vol 993, p 3, 16 December 1966 (ICESCR).

8 UN General Assembly, *International Covenant on Civil and Political Rights*, UNTS, vol 999, p 171, 16 December 1966 (ICCPR).

9 Australia, Canada, New Zealand and the United States, arguably the most relevant postcolonial countries, voted against UNDRIP: See 'An Inquiry into the Application of the United Nations Declaration on the Rights of Indigenous Peoples (UNDRIP) in Australia', *Parliament of Australia* (Report) [3.2] <https://www.aph.gov.au/Parliamentary_Business/Committees/Joint/Aboriginal_and_Torres_Strait_Islander_Affairs/UNDRIP/Report/Chapter_3_-_International_Applications_of_UNDRIP>. They later relented. After the Truth and Reconciliation Commission delivered its report (see Chapter 6), Canada has most obviously sought to comply with UNDRIP. In New Zealand, the National-led coalition government elected in 2023 includes two minor parties which seek to rescind New Zealand's accession to the Declaration. Ironically, a previous National government (2008–17), rather than a more progressive administration, ratified UNDRIP.

10 See UN General Assembly, *United Nations Declaration on the Rights of Indigenous Peoples*: resolution/adopted by the General Assembly, A/RES/61/295, 2 October 2007 (UNDRIP).

11 Ireland, South Africa, the United Kingdom and the United States have also ratified UNDRIP. The positions of First Nations in Canada and the United States are comparable. See generally, Miriam Jorgensen (ed), *Rebuilding Native Nations: Strategies for Governance and Development*

regulatory perspective because they have UK-heritage legal systems, but cannot be considered human rights States, since neither China nor Singapore has ratified both the ICCPR and ICESCR.

The specific statutory provisions and regulatory arrangements of UK-heritage countries are different; sometimes significantly so. Nevertheless, it is plausible to identify and build on Anglophone traditions in the regulation of companies.[12] Since these States have undertaken to respect, protect and fulfil their citizens' human rights, it is also reasonable to consider their corporate regulatory systems in the context of their human rights undertakings.

The other major English-speaking common law tradition evolved in the United States, whose Supreme Court has exercised an important influence on the development of corporate law. While I will refer to some key Supreme Court decisions and theories of the corporation which have found strong traction in the United States, consideration of US law and its context will be tangential. Not only has the United States not ratified ICESCR, Supreme Court decisions, notably *Santa Clara County*,[13] *Citizens United*[14] and *Hobby Lobby*,[15] are incompatible with the ideas presented about human rights and duties, and, to the extent practicable, exclusion of bodies corporate from the scheme of human rights.[16] Furthermore, seats of registration, such as Delaware and Wyoming, which may compete with each other in their laxity and opacity of regulation, present incompatible regulatory models to the one this study promotes.

Humanism fundamentally informs this study. A precise definition of the term 'humanism' is elusive and has changed over time, depending on the people, groups and movements claiming to act in its name.[17] Nevertheless, contemporary humanists are likely to recognise the following ideas:

(University of Arizona Press, 2007). Indeed, some First Nations identify all of North America as 'Turtle Island'. See William N Fenton, 'This Island, the World on the Turtle's Back' (1962) 75(298) *Journal of American Folklore* 283.

The settler population in South Africa is economically dominant but not supernumerary. See David Thomas, 'Is South African transformation dead?' *African Business* (Web Page, 1 September 2020) <https://african.business/2020/09/economy/black-economic-power-matters-is-south-african-transformation-dead>. The issue of 'race' remains highly controversial in South Africa. For the 2022 Census, Statistics South Africa did not distinguish between Black Africans and Khoisan, who are the first Indigenous Peoples of the country and today comprise a small minority.

12 Under the Irish Constitution, Irish is the country's first official language. See *Constitution of Ireland 1937* (Ireland) art 8. English and French have equal legal status in Canada. See *Constitution Acts 1867* (Canada) art 133. English is one of the 11 official languages of South Africa. See *Constitution of the Republic of South Africa 1996* (South Africa) s 6.

13 See *Santa Clara County v Southern Pacific Railroad Company* 118 US 394 (1886).

14 See *Citizens United* (n 1).

15 See *Burwell v Hobby Lobby Stores, Inc* 573 US 682 (2014).

16 The United States has signed but not ratified ICESCR.

17 See Tony Davies, *Humanism* (Routledge, 1997) 1–6.

> Humanism … affirms the worth, dignity and autonomy of the individual and the right of every human being to the greatest possible freedom compatible with the rights of others. Humanists have a duty of care to all of humanity including future generations. Humanists believe that morality is an intrinsic part of human nature based on understanding and a concern for others … Humanism aims at the fullest possible development of every human being. It holds that democracy and human development are matters of right … Humanism insists that personal liberty must be combined with social responsibility. Humanism ventures to build a world on the idea of the free person responsible to society, and recognises our dependence on and responsibility for the natural world.[18]

This study does not engage with claims that animals, machines or features of the natural environment should be included within the scope of human rights. Despite this Western humanist orientation, it is submitted that animals and the environment should be accorded the highest ethical, legal and regulatory consideration – they simply cannot claim human rights or assume responsibilities. For many Indigenous Peoples, drawing distinctions between humans and their immediate ecosphere might be considered absurd.[19] I note and respect that perspective, but its examination lies beyond the range of this study. Nevertheless, it is critical that we recognise ourselves as part of and situated within Nature,[20] otherwise claims for sustainability lack cogency.

I also argue that machines, however complex they may be, are instruments for human benefit and nothing more. Corporations fall into this category of tools to be used for human social and economic benefit. At first face, then, because bodies corporate do not possess human dignity, they are excluded from the human rights ecosystem. Nevertheless, it may be necessary to include them instrumentally to ensure that the property rights of human beings are respected, and generally to guarantee the rule of law in a business context.

1.1 Aim

The primary aim of this study is to present a model of company regulation that is fully consonant with the protection, respect for and fulfilment of human

18 See Humanists International, *Amsterdam Declaration* (Web Page) <https://humanists.international/what-is-humanism/the-amsterdam-declaration>.

19 See eg, 'Indigenous people and nature: a tradition of conservation', *UN Environmental Programme* (Web Page, 26 April 2017) <https://www.unep.org/news-and-stories/story/indigenous-people-and-nature-tradition-conservation>; Rachel Evans, 'What if whales took us to court? A move to grant them legal personhood would include the right to sue', *The Conversation* (Web Page, 15 April 2024) <https://theconversation.com/what-if-whales-took-us-to-court-a-move-to-grant-them-legal-personhood-would-include-the-right-to-sue-227335>.

20 See Paul-Henri d'Holbach cited by Richard Norman, *On Humanism* (Routledge, 2004) 11–12.

rights. Public lawyers tend to identify 'regulations' as primary, secondary or even tertiary legislation but legislation nonetheless.[21] This study adopts a broader conception. Indeed, the term 'regulation' is used because, beyond a specific legal perspective, its precise meaning is fluid, and therefore permits a pragmatic, multidisciplinary consideration of policy, law, subordinate legislation, oversight practices, soft law and other measures for limiting or authorising public or private conduct to promote social goals in the field of corporations.[22]

1.2 A neo-concessionist model

Concessionism is generally portrayed as one of the theories that seek to explain the company as a juristic person.[23] Competing explanations include organic (real) and contract theories.[24] I question whether concessionism is, indeed, a theory, and propose instead that it is an observable regulatory practice. In its lack of theoretical specificity, concessionism may be likened to pragmatism, which itself may be characterised as a method of inquiry that searches for a workable truth, rather than a theory.[25] This study uses a pragmatic method.

It is a matter of observable fact that, historically, commercial companies – as opposed to, say, the ancient collegium – could only gain legal status by grant of the sovereign or, in recent times, the State. Today, while the requirements for registration of a company tend to be minimal, corporators may only establish a company if they comply with the rules set by the legislature and overseen by a regulator.

One commentator sums up the concessionist position as 'if the state makes available the possibility of incorporation it is entitled to ask for something in return'.[26] No doubt, historically, a particular group of corporators was permitted to form a body corporate, such as the East India Company, because the State was likely to gain identifiable financial benefits.[27] Today, corporators are not required to justify the formation of a company on the grounds of an identifiable economic or social benefit. And so, rather than characterising the

21 See eg, Petra Butler, 'Rights and Regulation' in Susy Frankel (ed), *Learning from the Past, Adapting for the Future: Regulatory Reform in New Zealand* (LexisNexis, 2011) 241, 241.

22 Cf Cass R Sunstein, *Valuing Life: Humanizing the Regulatory State* (University of Chicago Press, 2014).

23 See eg, RWM Dias, *Jurisprudence* (4th ed, Butterworths, 1976) 358.

24 For a useful discussion of principal theories and an explanation of her own thesis, see Eva Micheler, *Company Law: A Real Entity Theory* (Oxford University Press, 2017) ch 1.

25 Catherine Legg and Christopher Hookway, 'Pragmatism' in Edward N Zalta (ed), *The Stanford Encyclopedia of Philosophy* (Summer 2021 ed) <https://plato.stanford.edu/archives/sum2021/entries/pragmatism/>.

26 See Micheler (n 24) 17.

27 See generally, Susan Watson, *The Making of the Modern Company* (Hart Publishing, 2022).

concession of incorporation as a matter of quid pro quo, it may be seen as an exercise in contextualisation. The political community which permits incorporation provides the ethical, legal and regulatory ecosystem in which a company is permitted to exist and operate. The political communities considered in this study are human rights States.

A concessionist proposition goes no further than establishing that the State permits the incorporation of companies and broadly prescribes their basic structure, such as having shares and directors. This legal fact does not ascribe a particular theory to the company and does not exclude or necessarily favour features of organic, contract or enterprise conceptions and does not prescribe organisational structures. New Zealand, for example, does not distinguish between proprietary (private) and public companies, and therefore leaves it to corporators to craft constitutions and establish arrangements that are appropriate for, say, a one-person or a widely held company.

Jettisoning some historical baggage but reasserting the principle of State concession, the corporate regulation model presented in this study is identified as 'neo-concession'. This model seeks to meld the State's unique power to grant legal personality (and limited investor liability) with its comprehensive human rights obligations. Due to the context of the human rights State in which incorporation is permitted, it is implicit in this model that corporations assume obligations, at minimum, to respect human rights,[28] whereas corporate actors, such as directors and shareholders, are expected to be 'competent citizens' who understand and act in accordance with their situation in a human rights-informed political community.

This neo-concession model might suggest authoritarianism but that is neither intended nor necessary. The model – perhaps idealistically – envisages regulation operating in a cooperative democracy in which most legal actors, whether individuals, associations or corporations controlled by individuals share broad common goals and practices, and disagreement is agonistic, rather than antagonistic. Of course, some citizens will fail to recognise their situatedness in a particular political community and will not comply with their social duties.[29] Likewise, some corporate actors, including their advisors, will abuse the grant of legal personality and limited liability; nevertheless the model is informed by primary presumptions of community cooperation and citizen competence.[30]

28 See 'Protect, Respect and Remedy: a Framework for Business and Human Rights: Report of the Special Representative of the Secretary-General on the Issue of Human Rights and Transnational Corporations and Other Business Enterprises', A/HRC/8/5, UN Human Rights Council, 7 April 2008.

29 So-called 'sovereign citizens' eg, reject the authority of the State. See Mellie Ligon, 'The Sovereign Citizen Movement: A Comparative Analysis with Similar Foreign Movements and Takeaways for the United States Judicial System' (2021) 35(2) *Emory International Law Review* 297.

30 Cf Valerie Braithwaite, 'Closing the Gap between Regulation and the Community' in Peter Drahos (ed), *Regulatory Theory: Foundations and Applications* (ANU Press, 2017) 25.

Another feature of the context of this study is the existing free market economic system.[31] I do not uncritically support that system; indeed I believe that much might be gained from considering alternatives, such as cooperatives as business entities or Distributism as a means of allocating wealth and welfare,[32] since they may better promote human dignity, but these considerations lie beyond the scope of this study. And so, in using the term 'cooperative democracy', I seek to note the necessity of collaboration among people and the organisations they control or in which they hold a stake for the functioning of a political community, and do not propose a radical restructuring of the economic system. The concept of 'Regulatory Capitalism', which 'offers the vision of private wealth-creating corporations that are also legally and arguably, socially accountable',[33] corresponds with the aims of this study.

1.3 Structure

After this introduction, the study is divided into six linked but potentially freestanding chapters and a conclusion.

1.3.1 Human rights and duties, and corporations

Chapter 2 outlines key UN human rights instruments and identifies UN initiatives that have special relevance to companies. Principal emphasis lies with the UDHR, with particular attention being paid to art 29 which affirms citizen duties. This is a critical provision which is often overlooked but is crucial in establishing the overall scheme of human rights and responsibilities that is dependent on reciprocity within a political community.

Affirmations of human rights are both normative, since they record the empirical requirements of full human flourishing, and aspirational because many people live in countries in which those expectations are not currently realised. The States considered in this study can, however, be expected to fully honour their human rights obligations, and these obligations should inform company regulation.

31 For a discussion of the difference between a free market (transparent and open, with a diffusion of power) and capitalism (opaque and monopolistic, with concentrations of power), see Immanuel Wallerstein, 'Braudel on Capitalism, or Everything Upside Down' (1991) 63(2) *Journal of Modern History* 354.

32 See eg, Alexander William Salter, *The Political Economy of Distributism: Property, Liberty, and the Common Good* (Catholic University of America Press, 2023).

33 See Iris H-Y Chiu, 'An Institutional Theory of Corporate Regulation' (2018) 71(1) *Current Legal Problems* 279. On Regulatory Capitalism in general, see John Braithwaite, *Regulatory Capitalism: How It Works, Ideas for Making It Work Better* (Edward Elgar, 2008); David Levi-Faur, 'Regulatory Capitalism' in Peter Drahos (ed), *Regulatory Theory: Foundations and Applications* (ANU Press, 2017).

1.3.2 Concession to neo-concession

In Chapter 3, I argue that commercial enterprises have only ever gained legal personality through concession of the sovereign or the State. That concession has always been contextual, such as the need for a State to fund war.[34] While a company may no longer require a royal charter, the simplified registration process of a company remains a concession of the State and should be understood in the context of the human rights obligations the State has undertaken to protect and fulfil.

This chapter argues for a pragmatic approach to the corporation as a legal entity and dismisses claims that purport to provide a unified theory of the company. Rather, we need to concentrate on what society needs from business vehicles and what works best, including promoting sustainable wealth generation and respect for human rights and duties.

Provided one accepts the State has some prerogative to interfere in individual arrangements, concessionism as a practice can make claims for ideological neutrality. The proposal of neo-concessionism, however, is not ideologically neutral and better aligns with other progressive proposals than laissez-faire models.[35] This chapter identifies some of these proposals and outlines their compatibility with a neo-concession approach.

1.3.3 Companies Acts and legislative considerateness

Chapter 4 considers the legislation that governs companies. At a minimum that legislation should be proportionate and duly enacted in accordance with the rule of law; manifest 'internal morality';[36] be consonant with the State's duty to promote human rights; and meet the needs of society in general.

Most companies, in number but not economic power, are small and medium enterprises (SMEs).[37] Many SMEs are likely to be incorporated partnerships in substance and so do not correspond with theories of the corporation and models that inform companies legislation. The legislature needs to ensure laws meet the needs of all entrepreneurs and corporate stakeholders.

34 See generally, Watson (n 27).

35 See generally, Lawrence E Mitchell, *Progressive Corporate Law* (Routledge, 1996) and specifically, Lewis D Solomon, 'On The Frontier of Capitalism: Implementation of Humanomics by Modern Publicly Held Corporations: A Critical Assessment' (1993) 50(4) *Washington and Lee Law Review* 1625.

36 See Lon L Fuller, *The Morality of Law* (rev ed, Yale University Press, 1969); Cass R Sunstein and Adrian Vermeule, 'The Morality of Administrative Law' (2018) 131(7) *Harvard Law Review* 1924.

37 In New Zealand eg, roughly 97% of businesses are SMEs. See 'Small business', *Ministry of Business, Innovation and Employment* (Web Page, 2024) <www.mbie.govt.nz>.

Directors' duties, in particular the fundamental duty of loyalty, originated in trust law. Do the rules of equity meet the needs of the modern corporation? This chapter argues for a reassessment of the role of directors and their duties and proposes a statement of principles on directors' duties that is not path dependent on trust law and suits the needs of direct and indirect stakeholders. Furthermore, only humans should be permitted to be corporate directors.[38] (The issue of non-human directors is considered further in Chapter 7.)

A corollary of granting legal personality is the State's right to suspend a company's separate existence, ignore that legal existence or remove it from the register of companies under appropriate circumstances. (The courts may also pierce the corporate veil under limited and uncertain circumstances.[39]) I raise the question whether an abuse of legal personality provision akin to general anti-avoidance provisions in tax legislation should be adopted.

1.3.4 The role of the corporate regulator – regulatory considerateness

Chapter 5 considers two aspects of the corporate regulator and their practice – institutional competence and regulatory considerateness.

In the traditional trifurcation of governmental powers, the legislature makes statutes, courts interpret laws and the executive administers laws. In the Westminster system such boundaries are fudged because Cabinet, made up of elected members of the majority party (or coalition members), generally decides which legislative proposals go before Parliament. Judges develop the common law and interpret statutes, but the regulator possesses significant practical power in applying those laws. The regulator most obviously administers the law but may have some discretion to issue low-level subordinate legislation. Furthermore, in practice, they have a quasi-judicial role since their interpretation of relevant legislation stands until someone is prepared to incur the costs of successfully challenging it in court. The regulator must comply with domestic human rights laws and, as an agent of the State, it is incumbent on them to further the State's international human rights promises. The first theme of the chapter, therefore, considers the institutional competence of the regulator, particularly their capacity to protect and promote human rights.

The second theme is considerateness for those who are governed by company law. Legislative considerateness, which is discussed in Chapter 4, is about how the legislature crafts governing statutes to be fit for purpose. A related concern is how the regulator can engage most effectively with those who must comply with company statutes. We can expect cooperation with

38 Cf UK corporate directors, corporate trustees and corporate general members of limited partnerships.

39 See Lord Sumption's analysis in *Prest v Petrodel Resources Ltd* [2013] UKSC 34.

corporations, industry bodies and advisors in developing regulations. The regulator also needs to understand the capacities of the people regulated and provide appropriate education and tools to aid compliance. Here I adapt a well-established but simplified pyramid approach to regulation.[40]

Both institutional competence and regulatory considerateness may require international cooperation but, conversely, the regulator should be permitted to refuse to cooperate with rogue jurisdictions.

1.3.5 Towards regulatory confederation

While all human rights are indivisible and interrelated, UNDRIP extrapolates and situates those rights to reflect the similar but specific experiences of Indigenous Peoples, who have been the subjects of colonisation. UNDRIP indicates ways of decolonising regulation within postcolonial countries.

A radical issue here lies with traditional State claims to unique and indivisible sovereignty being plausibly disputed by Indigenous Peoples within settler societies.[41] Concessionism is about the grant of privileges by the sovereign to its citizens, but what if the State does not have sovereignty over Indigenous Peoples because they never ceded sovereignty? A neo-concession approach embraces legal pluralism in corporate regulation.

In Chapter 6, I argue that settler majoritarian countries – Australia, Canada and New Zealand – should move towards some form of 'regulatory confederation', which entails ensuring corporate law, governance and regulation not only meet the needs of their Indigenous Peoples, but also fully respects their autonomy. Power-sharing is consonant with neo-concessionism because it takes proper account of Indigenous rights in the postcolonial context. Each of the three countries have made efforts to decolonise the regulation of Indigenous corporations and each can learn from each other's efforts, but far more work needs to be done before regulatory confederation or an arrangement that Indigenous People lead and co-create is achieved. Canada's Truth and Reconciliation Commission Report and its domestic legislation implementing UNDRIP provide important guidelines in this regard.

1.3.6 Corporate regulation and technology

A human being must never be an instrument for another's ends but a machine, however complex, is no more than a tool for achieving human objectives. Technological developments may provide useful ways to aid decision-making,

40 Cf Ian Ayres and John Braithwaite, *Responsive Regulation: Transcending the Deregulation Debate* (Oxford University Press, 1993).

41 See eg, Joseph P Kalt, 'The Role of Constitutions in Native Nations: Laying a Firm Foundation' in Miriam Jorgensen (ed), *Rebuilding Native Nations: Strategies for Governance and Development* (University of Arizona Press, 2007) 78.

but humans must make the ultimate corporate decisions. Chapter 7 outlines certain technological challenges to human autonomy and argues that human directors must continue to control and manage companies, and be held responsible for their acts and omissions.

Two specific technological developments are considered. These are code-based enterprises (CBEs) and forms of artificial intelligence (AI), either of which might be permitted to usurp the role of human directors. This chapter argues that corporate law and regulation must ensure human directorial autonomy and personal responsibility.

1.4 Concluding comments

The aims of this succinct monograph are ambitious and wide-ranging. The study does not claim to be exhaustive or canonical in any of the areas discussed but aims to raise questions and debate among lawmakers, policymakers, regulators, academics, students and anyone else who holds an interest in corporate law and regulation. While the golden thread of human rights and responsibilities is intended to bring coherence to the study, each of the six substantive chapters are designed to be freestanding and intellectually stimulating, and it is hoped may spur further study.

Despite holding the greatest regard for many of the company law theorists identified, I have sought to relegate theory to a marginal role. A particular theory may be implausible and fail to explain the company in the light of legal fact; another may explain business organisations in general and not specifically bodies corporate; while another may not be a theory in the usual sense of establishing concepts rather than describing practice. If we really care about how corporations exist and operate in the real world, we should focus on legal fact – as it is and how it might be – and business practice. Then we can engage with pursuing the constantly moving target of optimal regulation.

Each substantive chapter includes a key proposal or provocation. Chapter 2 rejects inclusion of corporations within the scope of human rights, other than as instruments for ensuring humans' rights. Chapter 3 marginalises broadly accepted theories of the company. Chapter 4 suggests a general statutory veil-piercing provision akin to the general anti-avoidance rule in tax law. Chapter 5 proposes a principle of regulatory considerateness for regulators dealing with incompetent corporators. Most importantly for Australia, Canada and New Zealand, Chapter 6 argues for the development of a regulatory confederation between the State and Indigenous Peoples in postcolonial societies so that those countries can fully comply with their UNDRIP undertakings. Chapter 7 adopts an approach to advanced technology that asserts the need for autonomous human directors, rejects recognition of CBEs without submission to regulation and supports hands-on, human-centric regulation of AI. In accordance with the overall study, this is not an instance of Luddite reaction but is rather an assertion of humanism in the contemporary context.

2 Human rights and corporations

2.1 Introduction

This section outlines the humanism that informs human rights, and considers rights and duties. Affirmations of universal human rights are then explained.

2.1.1 Humanism

The humanism that informs this study is 'founded on the belief in the irreducible dignity of humans, a belief in the efficacy and worth of human freedom and hence also human responsibility'.[1] Human existence is firstly distinguished by human dignity – the uniqueness of the embodied human mind. Indeed, the *Universal Declaration of Human Rights* (UDHR) art 1 affirms '[a]ll human beings are born free and equal in dignity and rights'. This affirmation of equal human dignity and rights of the embodied human person is the founding principle of universal human rights. Immanent dignity prohibits humans from ever being conceived as instruments of another or ends to 'greater' goals.[2]

The autonomous capacity to reason is 'most fundamental to the dignity and worth of human beings because it distinguishes humans from other animals and elevates them above the realm of causally determined nature'.[3] Historically, the concept of individual autonomy provided 'freedom to pursue personal goals and interests' but was always subject 'to the principle of not harming others or interfering with others' freedom'.[4]

1 See Richard A Cohen, 'Introduction' in Emmanuel Levinas, *Humanism of the Other*, tr N Poller (University of Illinois Press, 2003) i, ix.

2 See Samuel Kerstein, 'Treating Persons as Means' in Edward N Zalta and Uri Nodelman (eds), *The Stanford Encyclopedia of Philosophy* (Winter 2023 ed) <https://plato.stanford.edu/archives/win2023/entries/persons-means/>.

3 See Stephen Mulhall and Andrew Swift, *Liberals and Communitarians* (Blackwell, 1995) 43.

4 See Anthony Grayling, 'Social Evils and Social Good' in David Utting (ed), *Contemporary Social Evils* (Policy Press for Joseph Rowntree Foundation, 2009) 103, 105.

DOI: 10.4324/9781003509066-2

Aristotelian virtue ethics provides a useful way of explaining the social situatedness of the competent and cooperative citizen of the human rights State which is committed to the *International Bill of Human Rights* (IBHR).[5] In this scheme, universal justice is the 'whole of virtue in its other-regarding aspect' so that 'all branches of moral virtue involve our relations to others'.[6] Such talk of universal justice might suggest something metaphysical, above or beyond us, but is, in fact, something that should be present in every social interaction between people. Since empathy is the root of all ethics,[7] other-regarding virtue requires us to do 'what anyone filling such and such a role ought to do'.[8] People should be enabled to act virtuously or excellently in particular situations.

In our lives, we are interdependent with others.[9] We create meaning, including ethics and law, together, within political communities.[10] Once a political community has been formed, its members enjoy certain rights and owe their fellow community members duties or responsibilities, which are only realisable within that political community.[11] Intra-communal rights claims 'certify the veracity of mutual trust and of trust in the shared network that endorses and validates collective solidarity. "Belonging" translates as trust in the benefits of human solidarity, and in the institutions that arise from solidarity'.[12]

2.1.2 Rights and duties

The words denoting 'law', which carry a connotation of duty *and* right are the same in many languages.[13] The preambles to both the *International Covenant*

5 The IBHR comprises *Universal Declaration of Human Rights*, GA Res 217A (III), UN GAOR, UN Doc A/810 (10 December 1948) (UDHR), UN General Assembly, *International Covenant on Economic, Social and Cultural Rights*, UNTS, vol 993, p 3, 16 December 1966 (ICESCR) and UN General Assembly, *International Covenant on Civil and Political Rights*, UNTS, vol 999, p 171, 16 December 1966 (ICCPR).

6 See Lesley Brown, 'Introduction' in Aristotle, *The Nicomachean Ethics*, tr David Ross (Oxford University Press, 2009) i, xxiv.

7 See Bertrand Russell, *History of Western Philosophy and Its Connection with Political and Social Circumstances from the Earliest Times to the Present* (2nd ed, Routledge, 1961) 738.

8 See Alasdair MacIntyre, *After Virtue: A Study in Moral Theory* (3rd ed, Duckworth, 2007) 184.

9 See Martha Minow, *Applying Rights Rhetoric to Economic and Social Claims. Economic and Social Rights and the Right to Health* (Harvard University Press, 1995).

10 See Terry Eagleton, *Literary Theory: An Introduction* (University of Minnesota Press, 1983) 183.

11 On the paradox that universal human rights can only be realised within discrete political communities, see Hannah Arendt, *The Origins of Totalitarianism* (3rd ed, Harcourt, Brace, 1967) 291–92.

12 See Zygmunt Bauman, 'The Absence of Society' in David Utting (ed), *Contemporary Social Evils* (Policy Press for Joseph Rowntree Foundation, 2009) 149.

13 See HH Hahlo and Ellison Kahn, *The South African Legal System and Its Background* (Juta & Co, 1968) 76, fn 1.

on Civil and Political Rights (ICCPR) and the *International Covenant on Economic, Social and Cultural Rights* (ICESCR) state that 'the individual, having duties to other individuals and to the community to which he belongs, is under a responsibility to strive for the promotion and observance of the rights recognized in the present Covenant'. Rights and duties are both vertical (State-citizen) and horizontal (citizen-citizen) in their directions. Human rights and human duties are conjoined in a web of asymmetrical reciprocity, which includes and involves all members of the political community. Society respects human dignity when each person's particular 'capabilities for fully human functioning' or flourishing are developed.[14]

Because everyone is fundamentally similar, but each person's capabilities are different and fluid, the rights we may claim at a particular point in time and the responsibilities we owe are not directly proportionate. For example, due to their extreme vulnerability, people with severe mental incapacities may have significant rights claims, but they may be unable to take on significant responsibilities. Such asymmetry is in the nature of the scheme of human rights, which can be seen as a social pooling of shifting needs and abilities.

The responsibility component of human rights is a critical concern for this study: it is an important ground for asserting human centrality, given that only people can be moral agents, and contributes to the ethical basis for humanist corporate regulation by recognising that the people who control and hold stakes in a company owe duties to their fellow citizens and are not abstracted from greater society within a corporate cocoon.

While its title identifies a declaration of rights, the UDHR also includes a broadly worded duties affirmation. Art. 29(1) provides '[e]veryone has duties to the community in which alone the free and full development of his personality is possible'. Other declarations, notably the 1948 *American Declaration of the Rights and Duties of Man*,[15] include statements on a wide range of civic and social obligations, and list specific duties that approximately reciprocate the rights affirmed. For example, a right to social security on unemployment is matched by a duty to work.[16] Why does the UDHR not include a similar list of duties? Quite simply, during the prolonged negotiations over the UDHR, there 'was not enough time at the end to expand upon Article 29'.[17]

14 See Martha Nussbaum, 'Women and Equality: The Capabilities Approach' (1999) 138(3) *International Labour Review* 227, 243.

15 See Inter-American Commission on Human Rights (IACHR), *American Declaration of the Rights and Duties of Man*, 2 May 1948.

16 See ibid arts XVI and XXXVII.

17 See Johannes Morsink, *The Universal Declaration of Human Rights: Origins, Drafting, and Intent* (University of Pennsylvania Press, 1999) 240.

2.1.3 Universal human rights

Rights are 'ultimately grounded in the nature of things',[18] but are fleshed out through moral dialogue and political discourse,[19] that lead to the construction of moral megalogues. (A 'moral dialogue' is the process by which we identify shared fundamental values that guide our lives, and a 'moral megalogue' is a moral dialogue projected onto a larger scale.[20]) The affirmation of universal human rights in the UDHR is the greatest moral megalogue, which has 'inspired, and paved the way for, the adoption of more than seventy human rights treaties, applied today on a permanent basis at global and regional levels'.[21] Affirmations of human rights are both normative, since they record the empirical requirements of full human flourishing, and aspirational because many people live in countries in which those expectations are not currently realised. The economically developed States considered in this study can, however, be expected to fully honour their human rights obligations, and these obligations should inform social arrangements, including company regulation.

2.2 Human rights in law

Human rights are not in essence a legal concept, despite their most obvious expression in structural legal terms.[22] The ideals recorded in the UDHR were primarily intended to exert a moral and political influence on states, and promote a culture of human rights,[23] not to exhaustively prescribe the content of domestic laws.[24] In addition to the UDHR, the UNDRIP clarifies human rights in relation to Indigenous Peoples. Furthermore, according to the *Vienna Declaration and Programme of Action* (VDPA), 'it is the duty of States, regardless of their political, economic and cultural systems, to promote and protect all human rights and fundamental freedoms'.[25]

18 See AG Lehmann, *The European Heritage: An Outline of Western Culture* (Guild Publishing, 1984) 163.
19 See Jürgen Habermas, *Between Facts and Norms: Contributions to a Discourse Theory of Law and Democracy*, tr William Rehg (MIT Press, 1996) 457–58.
20 See Amitai Etzioni, 'Introduction' in Amitai Etzioni and David E Carney (eds), *Repentance: A Comparative Perspective* (Rowman & Littlefield, 1997) 1, 15.
21 See 'Universal Declaration of Human Rights', *United Nations* (Web Page) <https://www.un.org>.
22 See Stephen Toope, 'Cultural Diversity and Human Rights' (1997) 42 *McGill Law Journal* 169, 180.
23 See 'Joint Committee on Human Rights Sixth Report' (UK Parliament, 2003).
24 See Ian Brownlie, *Principles of Public International Law* (6th ed, Oxford University Press, 2003) 535.
25 See The World Conference on Human Rights, *Vienna Declaration and Programme of Action*, A/CONF.157/23, UN General Assembly, 12 July 1993, art 5.

Table 2.1 A comparison of domestic bills of rights

	Australia	*New Zealand*	*Canada*	*South Africa*
National bill of rights	No	Yes	Yes	Yes
Superior law	No	No	Yes	Yes
Entrenched law	No	No	Yes	Yes
Scope of rights	Electoral and ancillary	ICCPR	ICCPR (and confirmation of Indigenous rights)	ICCPR and ICESCR
Dimensions	Vertical	Vertical	Vertical	Vertical and horizontal

Under the UK-heritage dualist legal systems of Australia, Canada and New Zealand, international undertakings do not automatically have effect under domestic law, although courts typically seek to interpret domestic statutes in accordance with the international obligations undertaken by the State.[26] Table 2.1 indicates how selected countries have incorporated the IBHR into domestic law.

Australia may appear exceptional in not having a modern charter of rights at a federal level, although the state of Victoria and the Australian Capital Territory (ACT) have introduced their own charters. The *Commonwealth of Australia Constitution Act 1900* (Cth) includes electoral rights, from which the courts have developed freedom of (political) speech.[27] Bills of rights are not the only statutes that guarantee or promote human rights. Labour laws typically incorporate the International Labour Organization's Eight Fundamental Conventions.[28] Anti-discrimination laws also provide important rights protections, and some form of Human Rights Commission is usually charged with promoting all human rights in a country. Australia, for example, has four anti-discrimination Acts, and the *Australian Human Rights Commission Act 1986* (Cth) is designed to ensure effect is given to Australia's international human rights undertakings. Despite its lack of a bill of rights or an express constitution provision guaranteeing just administrative action, Australian administrative law influenced the right to just administrative action under the South African bill of rights and related legislation.[29]

26 See eg, *New Zealand Air Line Pilots' Association Inc v Attorney-General* [1997] 3 NZLR 269, 289.

27 See *Lange v Australian Broadcasting Corporation* (1997) HCA 25.

28 See 'Conventions and Recommendations', *International Labour Organization* (Web Page, 1996–2004) <https://www.ilo.org>.

29 See *Administrative Decisions (Judicial Review) Act 1977* (Cth) and *Promotion of Administrative Justice Act 2000* (South Africa). For a discussion, see Iain Currie and Jonathan Klaaren, *The Promotion of Administrative Justice Act Benchbook* (SiberInk, 2001) [2.7].

Neither the Canadian charter of rights and freedoms nor the *New Zealand Bill of Rights Act 1990* (NZBORA) expressly mentions citizens' duties or responsibilities but, since one of NZBORA's purposes is to affirm the country's commitment to the ICCPR, it implicitly incorporates the duties mentioned in that covenant (see ICCPR, preamble and art 19(3)). Victoria's *Charter of Human Rights and Responsibilities Act 2006* (Vic) provides that 'human rights come with responsibilities and must be exercised in a way that respects the human rights of others', for example, '[s]pecial duties and responsibilities are attached to the right of freedom of expression'. The preamble to the *Human Rights Act 2004* (ACT) includes the following purpose: 'This Act encourages individuals to see themselves, and each other, as the holders of rights, and as responsible for upholding the human rights of others'.

The key point here is that we may need to look in various places to find domestic rights and responsibilities, but, for the purposes of this study, we can rely on the relevant countries' internationally affirmed commitment to the IBHR, UNDRIP and VDPA.

2.3 Property

Property is a problematic rights issue, particularly in relation to companies. On the one hand, lacking human dignity, companies are implausible human rights claimants, but, on the other hand, they are typically formed to hold investors' proprietary interests.

Bills of rights tend neither to guarantee a certain level of property holdings, nor to prohibit existing property holdings from being extinguished, provided due process is followed. The *Magna Carta* (1215, 1297), which is commonly thought to guarantee extant property holdings under the common law, provides that '[n]o Freeman shall be ... disseised of his Freehold ... but by lawful Judgment of his Peers, or by the Law of the Land' (s 29). Similarly, UDHR art 17 provides that '[e]veryone has the right to own property' but adds '[n]o one shall be arbitrarily deprived of his property'. In other words, municipal law must not prohibit certain groups or individuals from owning property, but any existing property right may be extinguished, provided such action is in accordance with the rule of law,[30] which itself incorporates human rights principles.[31]

Excessive accumulation or abuse of property is socially undesirable but, from a human rights perspective, property is not an inherent 'bad'.

Individuals need 'some minimum amount of property in order to express their freedom by enforcing their will on external objects'.[32] Without access to some property an individual cannot realise their capacity for full human flourishing.

30 See eg, *Westco Lagan Ltd v Attorney-General* [2001] 1 NZLR 40.

31 See Tom Bingham, *The Rule of Law* (Penguin Books, 2011) 66–84.

32 See Liam Murphy and Thomas Nagel, *The Myth of Ownership: Taxes and Justice* (Oxford University Press, 2005) 45.

In the absence of a well-defined legal right or a sentiment of connection to land, people may not consider that they owe any duties of conservation. The influential article 'The Tragedy of the Commons' presented a model for explaining how multiple, self-interested individuals might ultimately deplete a shared limited resource, despite such an outcome being contrary to everyone's long-term interest.[33] The argument presented was ideologically charged and methodologically flawed;[34] nevertheless it is plausible that, without an identifiable owner or guardian, the quality of land or other property may deteriorate under certain circumstances. Holding communal land via a single legal person may be an appropriate way of sustaining that land, especially through generations.

For Indigenous Peoples, '[p]roperty constitutes the access to the material resources and territorial control that is essential to any real community'.[35] Intergenerational communal property might usefully be held in some form of corporation that meets the needs and complies with the customs of particular Peoples.

Nevertheless, corporate property ownership can be a social bad. Intellectual property rights (IPRs) are increasingly the most important type of business asset,[36] and, while their exact scope is debatable,[37] IPRs are also generally considered to be human rights.[38] Many jurisdictions include corporate property rights within their human rights schemes.[39] In Australia, tobacco companies seeking to protect their IPRs have challenged the government's public health policies.[40] While the tobacco companies did not argue that their human rights

33 See G Hardin, 'The Tragedy of the Commons' (1968) 162(3859) *Science* 1243.

34 Susan Jane Buck Cox, 'No Tragedy on the Commons' (1985) 7(1) *Environmental Ethics* 49.

35 See Nomi Stolzenberg, 'The Culture of Property' in R Schweder, M Minow and H Markus (eds), *Engaging with Cultural Differences: The Multicultural Challenge in Liberal Democracies* (Sage Foundation, 2002) 177, 180.

36 See 'Why Intellectual Property is Essential for your Business', http://www.wipo.int/sme/en/

37 See generally, Laurence R Helfer and Graeme W Austin, *Human Rights and Intellectual Property: Mapping the Global Interface* (Cambridge University Press, 2011).

38 UDHR art 27(2) provides: 'Everyone has the right to the protection of the moral and material interests resulting from any scientific, literary or artistic production of which he is the author'. ICESCR art 15, ICCPR art 19, the VDPA and other international and regional instruments confirm intellectual property rights as human rights. See World Intellectual Property Organization in collaboration with the Office of the United Nations High Commissioner for Human Rights, *Intellectual Property and Human Rights* (Report, 1998) <https://www.wipo.int/edocs/pubdocs/en/intproperty/762/wipo_pub_762.pdf.

39 See eg, Protocol 1 to the *European Convention for the Protection of Human Rights and Fundamental Freedoms* ETS 9 (20 March 1952) art 1 (ECHR).

40 See eg, Becky Freeman, Ross Mackenzie and Mike Daube, 'Should Tobacco and Alcohol Companies Be Allowed to Influence Australia's National Drug Strategy?' (2017) 27(2) *Public Health Research & Practice* <https://doaj.org/article/54c34fb9c3734550b54ed60f0e334a2a>.

had been denied,[41] in jurisdictions, including New Zealand, whose bills of rights extend human rights to juristic persons,[42] such claims have been made.[43]

2.4 Corporate claims to human rights

Despite the existential and moral implausibility of companies claiming human rights, various conventions and charters have extended rights to them.

The Council of Europe's *European Convention for the Protection of Human Rights and Fundamental Freedoms* (ECHR) does not expressly include non-natural persons within the ambit of affirmed rights,[44] but art 34, which defines who may apply to the European Court of Human Rights (ECtHR), identifies 'any person, non-governmental organization or group of individuals'. This provision appears to refer to representative bodies, such as the Red Cross pursuing the interests of prisoners of war. Had the intention been to include commercial corporations as direct rights-holders, one would expect an unambiguous statement.

In *Sunday Times v United Kingdom*,[45] which concerned art 10 (the right to freedom of expression), the ECtHR did not discuss whether a commercial body corporate itself could claim ECHR rights. The judgment referred to the '*Sunday Times*' but not to News Corporation, the multi-national corporate owner of that masthead. The court may have conceived the newspaper as an unincorporated body that represented the views of the journalists and editors, rather than the proprietary interests of shareholders. Since freedom of expression includes the right to impart and receive information, as well as the newspaper's journalists having a right to impart their findings, the public had a right to read them. The investigation into the disabling thalidomide drug manifested a critical public interest. Furthermore, since the crucial role of the Fourth Estate in a democracy has long been recognised,[46] it would have been a regressive, anti-democratic and highly legalistic decision not to recognise freedom of expression in this situation.

41 See *JT International SA v Commonwealth of Australia, British American Tobacco Australasia Limited v The Commonwealth* [2012] HCA 43; (2012) 291 ALR 669.

42 NZBORA s 29 provides: 'Except where the provisions of this Bill of Rights otherwise provide, the provisions of this Bill of Rights apply, so far as practicable, for the benefit of all legal persons as well as for the benefit of all natural persons'.

43 See eg, British American Tobacco New Zealand, 'Proposal to Introduce Plain Packaging of Tobacco Products in New Zealand: Submission by British American Tobacco (New Zealand) Limited' AgreeDisagree.co.nz (2013) [4.35].

44 See ECHR (n 39).

45 See *Sunday Times v United Kingdom*, application no 6538/74, judgment dated 26 April 1979 ('*Sunday Times*').

46 See eg, Gerard Brennan, 'The Third Branch and the Fourth Estate' (1997) 32 *Irish Jurist* 62.

While standing to pursue an action in the court may be ambiguous in relation to the full panoply of rights, the first protocol to the ECHR provides: 'Every natural *or legal* person is entitled to the peaceful enjoyment of his possession'.[47] In *Yukos v Russia*,[48] Yukos, a giant petroleum extraction company, was the subject of arbitrary tax audits and nationalisation of a crucial subsidiary, carried out in a way that violated the right to peaceful enjoyment of its property, as guaranteed by ECHR Protocol 1, art 1. The ECtHR generally seems to have conflated the interests of the shareholders and those of the company. It is significant that, in a partly dissenting opinion, it was noted, 'a legal entity as a legal institution, that is, as a product of legal techniques, a legal fiction, ultimately serves to represent the interests of certain individuals' and that shareholders could claim for the damage caused to the (insolvent) company.[49]

Both the *Sunday Times* and *Yukos* decisions can be seen as indirectly protecting individuals' rights through the instrument of a company. However, in *Société Cola Est v France*,[50] the ECtHR held that art 8 (right to respect for private and family life) could apply to a company's business premises. Protecting corporate privacy is less easily explained in instrumental terms but we can expect the rule of law to rein in the exercise of arbitrary and oppressive State power.

Corporations do not need to be included in the human rights calculus to achieve this end. But if they are included, that inclusion can only be partial due to their lack of corporeality. Such a cafeteria approach in selecting some rights but not others is incompatible with the principle affirmed in the VDPA that human rights are universal, indivisible, interdependent and interrelated.

2.4.1 Practical problems

Various practical problems arise when corporate claims to human rights are recognised.

Corporations may compete with vulnerable members of society who are most in need of human rights protections: for example, corporate claims to

47 Emphasis added. For a discussion, see Loukis Loucaides, *The European Convention on Human Rights: Collected Essays* (Brill, 2007). See also Marius Emberland, *The Human Rights of Companies: Exploring the Structure of ECHR Protection* (Oxford University Press, 2006); Andreas Kulick, 'Corporate Human Rights?' (2021) 32(2) *European Journal of International Law* 537; see also Andrew Clapham, *Human Rights and Non-State Actors* (Edward Elgar, 2013). The European Council includes 46 states.

48 See *OAO Neftyanaya Kompaniya Yukos v Russia*, application no 14902/04, judgment dated 31 July 2014, para 613 ('*Yukos*').

49 See ibid. Judge Bushev, joined in part by Judge Hajiyev [4.3] and [4.4].

50 See *Société Colas Est v France*, application no 37971/97, judgment dated 16 April 2002.

intellectual property rights may clash with Indigenous cultural rights.[51] More generally, rights can only be given effect in a context of budgetary constraint.[52] Finite financial, institutional and human resources for, say, promoting access to justice should be equitably distributed among all rights claimants. When a corporation successfully makes a claim against these limited resources in the context of criminal prosecution,[53] an individual, whose corporeality makes imprisonment possible, may be denied access to justice.

Corporations increasingly play the role of agents for delivery of basic human rights, such as security and water.[54] It is incongruous that a for-profit organisation performing quasi-State functions should be treated as a human rights-bearing 'citizen'. Corporations also mediate in a quasi-State way between different interest groups: for example, between the ostensibly competing expectations of consumers and employees. In performing these functions companies are not subject to democratic censure or judicial or ombud review in the way a government agency may be.

2.4.2 Interpretive problems

How can a legal construct be accorded rights that arise from the socially situated dignity of the embodied human person?

Despite its explicit grounding in human dignity, the *Constitution (South Africa) Act 1996* s 8(4) extends rights to juristic persons 'to the extent required by the nature of the rights and the nature of the juristic person'. (Trade unions, non-governmental organisations and religious groups, among other juristic persons, played a major role in opposing apartheid in South Africa and were subject to arbitrary and oppressive State action.[55]) In interpreting the bill of rights, the South African Constitutional Court (SACC) appears to view companies as inferior rights bearers.

In *Hyundai*,[56] having confirmed that juristic persons do not possess the human dignity from which a right to privacy is derived, the SACC continued, '[t]heir privacy rights, therefore, can never be as intense as those of human

51 On the incompatibility of collective cultural heritage and individuated intellectual property rights, see eg, Paul Hunt, 'Reflections on International Human Rights Law and Cultural Rights' in Margaret Wilson and Paul Hunt (eds), *Culture, Rights, and Cultural Rights: Perspectives from the South Pacific* (Huia, 2000) 25, 39–41.

52 See *Soobramoney v Minister of Health (KwaZulu Natal)* 1998 (1) SA 765 (CC) ('*Soobramoney*').

53 See eg, *Re Wiseline Corporation Ltd* (2002) 16 PRNZ 347 (CA).

54 See generally, Vandana Shiva, *Water Wars: Privatization, Pollution and Profit* (Southend Press, 2002).

55 See eg, Daryl Glaser, 'South Africa and the Limits of Civil Society' (1997) 23(1) *Journal of Southern African Studies* 5.

56 See *Investigating Directorate: SEO v Hyundai Motor Distributors (Pty) Ltd* [2000] ZACC 12 ('*Hyundai*').

beings. However, this does not mean that juristic persons are not protected by the right to privacy'.[57] However, this limited corporate privacy claim was instrumentally derived from concerns for democracy and social order.[58]

In *First National Bank*,[59] the SACC considered whether companies were entitled to property rights. (*Constitution (South Africa)* s 25(1) provides: 'No one may be deprived of property except in terms of law of general application, and no law may permit arbitrary deprivation of property'.) The SACC seemed to conceive companies' property rights as instruments for realising human interests. Concerns were shown for the disruptive effects on society, particularly shareholders and creditors, if companies' property rights were not recognised. Ultimately, the court reasoned that '[t]he property rights of natural persons can only be fully and properly realised if such rights are afforded to companies as well as natural persons'.[60] But, if the court was prepared to perceptually pierce the corporate veil in search of shareholders' interests, would it have been more consistent with humanism to recognise public companies as representative litigants?

2.4.3 Learning from the United States

The preambles to the three instruments that constitute the IBHR foreground the fundamental human rights principle of respect for equal human dignity. The United States' much older bill of rights does not explicitly espouse human dignity, but its informing natural rights doctrine appears compatible with later declarations of rights that are expressly based on human dignity.[61] Indeed, indicating inherent and indefeasible human dignity, the United States' bill of rights has been described as 'a series of definitions of things which could not be exchanged'.[62] Companies are deemed to be juristic persons, but, since they do not possess human dignity, can they claim natural (human) rights?

57 See ibid [18] (footnote omitted).

58 See ibid.

59 See *First National Bank of South Africa v Commissioner, SARS* [2002] ZACC 5 ('*First National Bank*').

60 See ibid [45].

61 On the influence of natural law on American constitutions, see Philip A Hamburger, 'Natural Rights, Natural Law, and American Constitutions' (1993) 102 *Yale Law Journal* 907. For a discussion of dignity in US rights jurisprudence, see Neomi Rao, 'Three Concepts of Dignity in Constitutional Law' (2013) 86 *Notre Dame Law Review* 183. Retired Supreme Court Justice Anthony Kennedy 'invoked repeatedly' dignity in his opinions – three times in *Lawrence v Texas* and nine times in *Obergefell v Hodges*, even though the word 'does not appear in the Constitution'. See Jeffrey Toobin, 'After Kennedy' *The New Yorker* (New York, 9 July 2018) 19.

62 See Arthur Okun cited by Geoff Mulgan, *Connexity: How to Live in a Connected World* (Chatto & Windus, 1997) 64. But budgetary decisions do need to be made that could be a matter of life or death. See eg, *Soobramoney* (n 52).

The US Supreme Court decisions in *Hobby Lobby*[63] and *Citizens United*[64] are not only markedly pro-business, they are also consistent with the extraordinary precedent established in *Santa Clara County* in approving corporate claims to ostensibly human rights.[65] Before

> the introduction of organic language into legal debates in 1880s, American courts had adhered to the 1819 Supreme Court decision in *Dartmouth College*[66] declaring a corporation to be 'an artificial being' and 'mere creature of law.' … in *Santa Clara County* ... the Supreme Court abruptly shifted gears to recognise corporations *as natural persons*.[67]

In *Hobby Lobby*, particular religious beliefs and the right to practise those beliefs were imputed to a company.[68] The decision was to the detriment of Hobby Lobby's tens of thousands of employees,[69] since those religious views impacted on the employees' reproductive health rights.[70]

In *Citizens United*, which arose from the Federal Electoral Commission's objection to a corporation using its economic power to traduce the reputation

63 See *Burwell v Hobby Lobby Stores, Inc* 573 US 682 (2014) ('*Hobby Lobby*').

64 See *Citizens United v Federal Electoral Commission* 558 US 310 (2010) ('*Citizens United*').

65 See *Santa Clara County v Southern Pacific Railroad Co* 118 US 394 (1886) ('*Santa Clara County*'). For a discussion of the decision and its consequences, see Thom Hartmann, *Unequal Protection: How Corporations Became "People" – And How You Can Fight Back* (2nd ed, Berrett-Koehler Publishers, 2010). In *Santa Clara County*, without discussion, the Supreme Court reportedly held that a corporation could access the equal protection guarantee under the 14th amendment to the US Constitution, which was introduced to protect ex-slaves. For a discussion of the context and purposes of the 14th amendment, see generally, Kurt T Lash, *The Fourteenth Amendment and the Privileges and Immunities of American Citizenship* (Cambridge University Press, 2014).

66 See *Dartmouth College v Woodward* 17 US 518 (1819).

67 See Amanda Porterfield, *Corporate Spirit: Religion and the Rise of the Modern Corporation* (Oxford University Press, 2018) 130 (emphasis added).

68 Cf Mocatta J's observation in *Rolloswin Investments*: 'A limited company is incapable of public worship or repairing to a church, or of exercising itself in the duties of piety and true religion, either publicly or privately, on any day of the week'. See *Rolloswin Investments Ltd v Chromolit Portugal Cutelarias e Produtos Metálicos SARL* [1970] 2 All ER 673, 675.

69 See Malcolm J Harkins III, 'The Uneasy Relationship of *Hobby Lobby*, *Conestoga Wood*, the Affordable Care Act, and the Corporate Person: How a Historical Myth Continues to Bedevil the Legal System' (2014) 7(2) *Saint Louis University Journal of Health Law & Policy* 201.

70 See *Hobby Lobby* (n 63) together with *Conestoga Wood Specialities Corp v Burwell* 573 US ___ (2014). The cases involved the interaction between the *Religious Freedom Restoration Act* of 1993, which prohibits government from substantially burdening a person's exercise of their religion, and regulations under the *Patient Protection and Affordable Health Care Act* of 2010. This latter Act requires employers to pay for their employee's health care insurance premiums for cover including reproductive health, such as the so-called 'morning after' pill. Hobby Lobby refused to pay for such cover on the grounds that it substantially burdened its exercise of religion.

of a progressive political candidate, an opinion concurring with the majority concluded 'to exclude or impede corporate speech is to muzzle the principal agents of the modern free economy. We should celebrate rather than condemn the addition of this speech to the public debate'.[71]

These decisions might be dismissed as manifestations of American exceptionalism, but victory in these cases could embolden corporate litigants in asserting their rights claims elsewhere and otherwise. This possibility is not nugatory in the light of Australia's experience of lawsuits and investor-state dispute settlement complaints[72] and New Zealand's affirming corporate claims to human rights.[73] In Canada, although they ultimately failed, companies have sought to rely on the country's Charter of Rights and Freedoms to claim a right to life,[74] freedom of religious belief to trade on Sundays[75] and freedom of expression to market cigarettes.[76]

The *Charter of Human Rights and Responsibilities Act 2006* (Vic)[77] and the *Human Rights Act 2004* (ACT)[78] reserve human rights to human beings, whereas NZBORA expressly includes juristic persons. NZBORA s 15 provides: 'Every person has the right to manifest that person's religion or belief in worship, observance, practice, or teaching, either individually or in community with others, and either in public or in private'. One leading text denies that legal persons can have religious beliefs,[79] but another suggests that 'churches and religiously associated organisations in the community' may have religious opinions.[80] While the authors' argument that, for example, the Catholic Church itself should be protected in asserting religious views seems sensible, it is not clear to which other religiously associated organisations that concession should apply – incorporated societies, say, the Society for the Promotion of Community Standards Inc, or limited liability companies, such as those underpinning the Seventh Day Adventist-run Sanitarium food business? In *Hobby Lobby*, once one legal person had been imputed a religious belief (a religiously oriented not-for-profit), the door was opened for commercial corporations to claim the same most human of rights.

71 See *Citizens United* (n 64) 9.

72 See eg, Joanna E Cohen et al., 'Plain Packaging of Tobacco Products: Lessons for the Next Round of Implementing Countries' (2020) 18 *Tobacco Induced Diseases* 94.

73 See NZBORA s 29.

74 See *Irwin Toy Ltd v Quebec (A-G)* (1989) 1 SCR 927.

75 See *R v Big M Drug Mart Ltd* [1985] 1 SCR 295. Cf *Hobby Lobby* (n 63).

76 See *RJR-MacDonald Inc v Attorney General of Canada* [1995] 3 SCR 199.

77 The Victorian Charter s 6 provides: 'Only persons have human rights'. In terms of section 3, '**person** means a human being'.

78 ACT Act s 6 provides: 'Only individuals have human rights'.

79 See Paul Rishworth et al., *The New Zealand Bill of Rights* (Oxford University Press, 2003) 112–13.

80 See Andrew Butler and Petra Butler, *The New Zealand Bill of Rights Act: A Commentary* (2nd ed, LexisNexis NZ, 2005) [5.11.6].

2.4.4 Rule of law

Since no particular conception of the rule of law has universal validity,[81] any government may claim observance with the rule of law, and may be justified in making such a claim, however eccentric its conceptions of justice may appear to an outsider.[82] When a State asserts its statutes and actions formally comply with the rule of law, nothing more is implied than adherence to its own constitutional rules. This is why inclusion of human rights within the rule of law is critical. The UDHR and later international instruments, including the ECHR, 'link protection of human rights with the rule of law'.[83] In the human rights era, a State cannot claim to follow the rule of law unless its laws substantively comply with and incorporate human rights.

Bills of rights invariably include provisions that support the rule of law, notably rights to natural justice and judicial review.[84] Because principles of natural justice and judicial review were developed to protect weak individuals against the power of the State,[85] it may be argued that corporations should not be able to claim those rights.[86] However, since the law permits the creation of companies with property and other rights necessary to carry on the enterprise,[87] it is incompatible with the rule of law to deny the corporation natural justice and judicial review if the State disrespects those rights. However, bills of rights are not legal codes. Indeed, they are rarely full statements of human rights. Companies operating in Victoria and ACT appear no more or less able to carry on business and protect their interests than those in states and territories without bills of rights or in New Zealand, which explicitly includes juristic persons within the ambit of NZBORA. In jurisdictions governed by the rule of law,[88] a guarantee in a bill of rights that, say, property rights may only be vitiated in accordance with the law is tautologous.

2.5 Concluding comments

Companies are not 'good corporate citizens';[89] they are mere instruments for achieving human ends and should not be *directly* included within the scope

81 See Wolfgang Friedman, *Law in a Changing Society* (2nd ed, Penguin Books, 1972) 500.

82 See Martin Weiser, 'North Korea: Law, but not as we know it' *theinterpreter* (Web Page, 25 November 2021) <https://www.lowyinstitute.org/the-interpreter/north-korea-law-not-we-know-it>.

83 See Bingham (n 31) 66.

84 See eg, NZBORA s 27(1) and (2).

85 See Doreen Lustig and JHH Weiler, 'Judicial Review in the Contemporary World – Retrospective and Prospective' (2018) 16(2) *International Journal of Constitutional Law* 315.

86 See Mark Bovens, 'The Corporate Republic: Complex Organizations and Citizenship' in Emilios A Christodoulides (ed), *Communitarianism and Citizenship* (Ashgate, 1998) 158, 162.

87 See eg, Corporations Act 2001 (Cth) s 124; Companies Act 1993 (NZ) s 16.

88 See generally, Bingham (n 31).

89 Cf *BCE v 1976 Debentureholders* [2008] 3 SCR 560.

of human rights. As a matter of legal convenience, they may be granted entity status and standing to pursue rights claims in their own names, but this should be seen as a form of representation, such as in the *Yukos* case where the unjust treatment of the company affected the shareholders' interests. Arguments that a corporation might hold, say, religious beliefs should, however, be robustly opposed. Conversely, if companies represent the interests of citizens of the human rights State, they can be expected to respect all human rights. If a corporation is a vehicle through which stakeholders indirectly assert their human rights, it must also be an instrument for them to perform their human rights duties. While legal persons are not moral agents in themselves, they exist and operate in the human moral sphere, and it is incumbent on those who control or otherwise influence corporate actions to ensure they simulate and comply with similar virtue expectations as people.

3 Concession to neo-concession

3.1 Introduction

Chapter 2 outlined relevant aspects of human rights. This chapter presents an argument that the human rights State provides the ethical and legal context in which companies are incorporated and are permitted to operate.[1] The broader context extends beyond the legal or civil capacity permitted by incorporation to include the general functional capacities of businesses (and the rules that determine those functions), and the capacities of organisations of which commercial corporations are a subset. Civil capacity relates to what a company may do because it is a company, whereas functional capacity concerns what any business may do.[2] For example, no domestic company, recognised foreign company, partnership or any other form of business organisation may sell recreational cannabis in Australasia, even if such an enterprise is legal in Canada. Broadly, I seek to marginalise traditional theories of the company to concentrate on what commercial corporations do in practice through the agency of human actors.

Concessionism has typically been coupled with the concept of the company as a fictive person and presented as a theory of legal personality. But what do we mean by a 'theory'? Various academic disciplines understand 'theory' differently, but general definitions include '[a]n explanation of a phenomenon arrived at through examination and contemplation of relevant facts' and '[t]he conceptual basis of a subject or area of study. Contrasted with practice'.[3] From these definitions, I submit that a proposition which does not explain the *specific* phenomenon under examination but rather explains more general phenomena or ignores relevant facts in its explanation is flawed as a theory. Various conceptual explanations of the company fail on these

1 Cf the concept of a corporate licence. See eg, Michelle Worthington and Peta Spender, 'Constructing Legal Personhood: Corporate Law's Legacy' (2021) 30(3) *Griffith Law Review* 348.

2 See 'Recognition of the Legal Personality of Foreign Commercial Corporations' (1928) 22(1) *American Journal of International Law* 157, 162.

3 See *Oxford English Dictionary* (online).

DOI: 10.4324/9781003509066-3

grounds. Furthermore, an explanation that simply identifies a practice is not a theory. Concessionism falls into this category.

The law deems a juristic person to be a legal actor separate from the human beings associated with it. Ownership of property may be attributed to this fictive legal person and it may nominally enter into contracts but, of course, cannot think, form an intention or do anything except through human actors. Arrangements and phenomena recognised as juristic persons range from universities, charitable trusts, trade unions, government ministries, some partnerships, massive commercial companies, one-person close corporations to deceased estates (in civil law jurisdictions). Given this variety, it seems implausible to construct an all-encompassing theory of juristic personhood beyond the most basic and tautologous observation that the law recognises juristic persons as such.

Is a narrower unifying theory of the commercial company plausible? Such theoretical claims are briefly discussed and critiqued below but I argue against the relevance of theory in favour of a pragmatic approach that recognises that companies can only be created by State concession. The role of corporate regulation is to ensure that the rules specific to companies are suitable and adequate for the context in which incorporation is granted. Once incorporated, companies are governed by an agglomeration of rules,[4] some of which apply to all companies and all relevant legal actors, while others depend on the provisions of particular corporate constitutions.

3.2 Some theories of the company

This section briefly identifies and critiques some prominent theories of the company.[5] The basic conceptions of the company are associated with clusters of ideas and ideologies, as illustrated in broad brushstroke in Table 3.1. (I discuss the cyberutopian approach in Chapter 7.[6])

4 See *Salomon v A Salomon & Co Ltd* [1896] UKHL 1 and *Meridian Global Funds Management Asia Ltd v Securities Commission* [1995] 3 NZLR 7 (PC) ('*Meridian Global*').

5 Team production theory may appear to be a significant omission from Table 3.1. See Margaret M Blair and Lynn A Stout, 'A Team Production Theory of Corporate Law' (1999) 85(2) *Virginia Law Review* 247. I see the team production model as an important counterpoint to contract theory, rather than a theory of the company. Nevertheless, the team production model seeks to reveal how businesses operate in practice: that approach represents an important link between legal and functional permissions.

6 The technologies discussed in Chapter 7 (code-based enterprises and artificial intelligence), while apparently dispensing with human autonomy, are initially determined by the agency of code writers and prompt engineers.

Table 3.1 Some basic concepts of the company compared

	Organic	*Contract*	*Neo-concession*	*Cyberutopian*
Basic philosophical position[a]	Conservative	Liberal	Communitarian-social liberal	Ultra-libertarian
Perception of the State	Fractal[b]	Promotes economic efficiency	Cooperative, enabling, trustworthy	Oppressive, intrusive, untrustworthy
Conception of freedom[c]	Negative; recognises duties	Negative	Positive and negative; recognises duties	Unrestrained
Role of corporate law	Recognise	Facilitate	Regulate	Barrier to freedom
Conception of company	Natural person	Web of contracts	Entity created by statute	Code
Ability to incorporate	Natural right	Legal formality	Concession/statutory prescription	Irrelevance

[a]On liberalism and communitarianism, see Stephen Mulhall and Adam Smith, *Liberals and Communitarians* (Blackwell, 1992). On the roots of conservatism as a political philosophy, see Edmund Burke, *Reflections on the Revolution in France* (Yale University Press, 2003, first published 1790). On libertarianism, see FA Hayek, *The Constitution of Liberty* (Routledge and Kegan Paul, 1976, first published 1960) and on ultra-libertarianism, see Ayn Rand, *Virtue of Selfishness: A New Concept of Egoism* (Centennial, 1964).

[b]In an organic view, individuals, associations and the State are elements of a naturally forming whole. See RWM Dias, *Jurisprudence* (4th ed, Butterworths, 1976) 527. An analogy may be drawn to fractals in mathematics for which each constitutive part of a phenomenon has the same statistical character as the whole. See Benoit B Mandelbrot, *Fractals: Form, Chance, and Dimension* (WH Freeman, 1977).

[c]See Isaiah Berlin, 'Two Concepts of Liberty' in Michael J Sandel (ed), *Liberalism and Its Critics* (Blackwell, 1984) 15. For Berlin, negative liberty is the right to be left alone by the State and others. Positive liberty consists of being able to do something, such as having an education, and typically requires government intervention.

3.2.1 Concession

Historically, corporators needed to demonstrate some identifiable public purpose before the sovereign or later the State would concede legal personality: 'the existence of incorporated activity was legitimated by a presumption of state-imposed controls on the scope of that activity'.[7] Even today, it may be argued that '[c]orporate personality exists merely for legal and business convenience'.[8] These statements do not contribute towards a concession theory of the corporation; they merely help to explain why and how in practice the State concedes legal personality.

From a concession perspective, the company is a statutory entity which the State allows people or other companies to create and provides the legislative means for doing so.[9] Legislation prescribes the conditions for incorporation and establishes the regulatory framework.[10] *Salomon's case* includes 'references that can be read as instances of concession theory. Lord Halsbury, for example, argued that the company is an "artificial creation",[11] and that "the law should recognise only that artificial existence"'.[12] I am not convinced these statements constitute a theory, rather than a method of statutory interpretation.

Corporators no longer need to demonstrate an identifiable public purpose but, despite the enactment of general incorporation statutes, a company may only be formed in accordance with the rules set by the legislature. While governing legislation allows for bespoke corporations, many rules are mandatory.[13]

Incorporation is the principal but not unique feature of concession, which is ongoing. A company must, for example, maintain certain essential requirements, such as having a shareholder and a director. If it fails to comply, its incorporation and status as a legal entity become forfeit. Furthermore, beyond the compliance requirements for obtaining and retaining incorporation, how concession is typically viewed *after* the corporation is registered is a matter of particular interest. In the traditional concession view, once created, 'limited liability entities have a responsibility to operate in the public interest'.[14]

7 See Stephen Bottomley, 'Taking Corporations Seriously: Some Considerations for Corporate Regulation' (1990) 19(3) *Federal Law Review* 203, 207 (footnotes omitted).

8 See ibid.

9 See ibid 206.

10 See Stefan J Padfield, 'Rehabilitating Concession Theory' (2014) 66 *Oklahoma Law Review* 327, 329–30.

11 See *Salomon* (n 4) 30.

12 See Bottomley (n 7) 207 (footnotes omitted).

13 Under Australian law eg, a company must have at least one member and a public company must have a company secretary. See *Corporations Act 2001* (Cth) ss 114 and 204A.

14 David L Cohen, 'Theories of the Corporation and the Limited Liability Company: How Should Courts and Legislatures Articulate Rules for Piercing the Veil, Fiduciary Responsibility and Securities Regulation for the Limited Liability Company' (1998) 51 *Oklahoma Law Review* 427, 444.

According to a commonly encountered narrative, the concession model was dominant for many years in English-speaking countries before being ousted by organic theory[15] and later contract-based conceptions. I am sceptical whether concessionism can accurately be described as a theory and prefer to see it as an observable regulatory practice. As such, claims for its demise are misplaced because, as matter of fact, people wishing to form a company in a particular jurisdiction must comply with the incorporation statute and administrative requirements of that State.

Concessionism tells us little about the nature of a company. This may explain why it is commonly linked to the fiction theory of the company in terms of which the legal person is a 'figment of our collective imagination',[16] albeit one dependent on State recognition.[17] Nevertheless, the need for compliance with legislation in order to incorporate does not imply a specific theory of the company.

All corporate theories are situated in a context of concessional practice. Before the *Joint Stock Companies Act 1844* (UK), entrepreneurs could not usually form a company; post-enactment, they could, albeit in accordance with statutory prescriptions. Furthermore, limited investor liability was not generally available prior to the *Limited Liability Act 1855* (UK);[18] soon afterwards, it became an ordinary investor expectation, even for shareholders in private companies.[19] A further feature of the modern company was established by the *Companies Act 1862* (UK), whose wording indicated that the company should have a separate existence from its members. 'Seen as a thing made by, but not of, people, the incorporated company was depersonalised and thus "completely separated" from its members.'[20] The modern corporation has, then, been created through a series of State concessions, as *Salomon's case* confirmed.[21] 'The sole guide must be the statute itself'.[22]

15 See eg, Amanda Porterfield, *Corporate Spirit: Religion and the Rise of the Modern Corporation* (Oxford University Press, 2018) 130.

16 See Yuval N Harari, *Sapiens: A Brief History of Humankind* (Vintage, 2014) 28.

17 See David H Bonham and Daniel A Soberman, 'The Nature of Corporate Personality' in Jacob S Ziegel (ed), *Studies in Canadian Company Law* (Butterworths, 1967) 5.

18 But see John Morley, 'The Common Law Corporation: The Power of the Trust in Anglo-American Business History' (2016) 116(8) *Columbia Law Review* 2145. Morley argues that the common law trust typically manifested substantially similar business features to the limited liability corporation.

19 See Otto Kahn-Freund, 'Reflections on Company Law Reform' (1944) 7(1/2) *Modern Law Review* 54.

20 See Paddy Ireland, Ian Grigg-Spall and Dave Kelly, 'The Conceptual Foundations of Modern Company Law' (1987) 14(1) *British Journal of Law and Society* 149, 150.

21 See *Salomon* (n 4). Cf the US Supreme Court's implicit acceptance of organic theory and the mystical baggage that carries in the contemporaneous *Santa Clara County v Southern Pacific Railroad Company*, 118 US 394 (1886).

22 See *Salomon* (n 4) 29.

The fact of concession is inconvenient for those who imagine the commercial corporation existing before or beyond the authorisation and control of a State bureaucracy. Claims that the commercial corporation could be created without State concession are counterfactual and implausible, but an organic or other conception is not incompatible with the practice of concession.

3.2.2 Organic

Organic, realist or natural entity theory,[23] which migrated from Germany to the United States in the late nineteenth century and has been implicitly revived in recent US Supreme Court decisions,[24] portrays corporations as naturally forming.[25] For organic theorists, '[t]he law does not create corporations but merely recognizes their independent existence'.[26] Juristic personality is automatic 'when a group reaches a certain level of organization, when it can make decisions and when it has a continuity of experience, regardless of whether the state accords it legal recognition'.[27] Drawing on the medieval concept of *corpus mysticum*,[28] organicists declared a corporation to be a natural body, indeed a 'natural person'.[29] From a humanist perspective, this proposition is implausible. The law constructs legal persons but only nature creates natural persons.

Organic theory presents a model of the corporation that some claim might have developed under the common law. This proposition may be rejected as an unprovable counterfactual claim. Nevertheless, if the legislative model of the company is radically different from an organic model, that divergence between norm and fact should give legislators and regulators pause for thought.

23 Arthur Machen's organic theory hints at this idea when he describes a corporation as a 'natural and spontaneous expression in figurative language of actual facts'. See Arthur W Machen Jr, 'Corporate Personality' (1910–11) 24(4) *Harvard Law Review* 253, 266.

24 See eg, Stefan J Padfield, 'The Silent Role of Corporate Theory in the Supreme Court's Campaign Finance Cases' (2013) 15(3) *University of Pennsylvania Journal of Constitutional Law* 831; Malcolm J Harkins III, 'The Uneasy Relationship of *Hobby Lobby*, *Conestoga Wood*, the Affordable Care Act, and the Corporate Person: How a Historical Myth Continues to Bedevil the Legal System' (2014) 7(2) *Saint Louis University Journal of Health Law & Policy* 201.

25 Cf the idea of autopoiesis or self-generation. See generally, Niklas Luhmann, *Law as a Social System*, tr A Ziegert (Oxford University Press, 2004).

26 Michael J Phillips, 'Reappraising the Real Entity Theory of the Corporation' (1994) 21(4) *Florida State University Law Review* 1061, 1068–69.

27 Ibid.

28 On the Christian church as a body (*corpus mysticum*) beyond an aggregation of adherents, see Brian Tierney, *Foundations of the Conciliar Theory: The Contribution of the Medieval Canonists from Gratian to the Great Schism* (Brill, 1997) 121–40.

29 See Porterfield (n 15) 160.

3.2.3 Contract

Contract theory, which provides the currently dominant US conception of the corporation,[30] envisages the company in much the same way as voluntary, common law and equitable arrangements, notably contracts, partnerships and trusts.[31] For the contractarian, incorporation merely stamps government approval on these ostensibly private arrangements.

Influenced by neo-classical economics,[32] in particular the doctrinaire approach prevalent at the University of Chicago from the 1970s,[33] contractarians dismiss statutory proclamations that the corporation is an entity but rather present it as a web of contracts. In this view, the corporation 'is nothing more than a legal fiction that serves as a nexus for a mass of contracts which various individuals have voluntarily entered into for mutual benefit'.[34] The primary contract is between the shareholders as principals and the managers as agents. Consequently the presumed aim of the shareholder to maximise wealth is given primacy.[35]

While the contractarian concept does not stand up to legal scrutiny, it does present a *theory* of the company in a way that concessionism (a regulatory practice) and real entity theory (see Section 3.2.4) do not. However, returning to the general definitions of 'theory', contractarianism fails to take account of relevant facts. In short, a company is not a web of contracts and directors are not legally agents of shareholders.[36] And so, while the model may appeal to neo-classical economists – and circularly the flawed theory may have influenced thinking on corporate law[37] – it is not consonant with the law of the real world, which is about predicting how courts will respond to a particular

30 For a critical discussion of contractarian theory, see William W Bratton Jr, 'The New Economic Theory of the Firm: Critical Perspectives from History' (1989) 41(6) *Stanford Law Review* 1471; William W Bratton Jr, 'The "Nexus of Contracts" Corporation: A Critical Appraisal' (1989) 74(3) *Cornell Law Review* 407.

31 See eg, Michael C Jensen and William H Meckling, 'Theory of the Firm: Managerial Behavior, Agency Costs and Ownership Structure' (1976) 3(4) *Journal of Financial Economics* 305.

32 See eg, R Neck, 'Neoclassical Economics: Origins, Evolution, and Critique' in D McCallum (ed), *The Palgrave Handbook of the History of Human Sciences* (Palgrave Macmillan, 2022).

33 See eg, Robert A Cord, *The Palgrave Companion to Chicago Economics* (Springer, 2023).

34 Daniel R Fischel, 'The Corporate Governance Movement' (1982) 35(6) *Vanderbilt Law Review* 1259, 1273.

35 For the seminal statement on shareholder primacy, see Milton Friedman, 'The Social Responsibility of Business Is to Increase Its Profits', *The New York Times* (New York, 13 September 1970) SM 17. For a critique, see eg, Andrew Keay, 'Shareholder Primacy in Corporate Law: Can It Survive? Should It Survive?' (2010) 7(3) *European Company and Financial Law Review* 369.

36 Contract theory does however take the principal-agency problem seriously, ie, how to prevent directors acting in their own interests. See eg, Kathleen M Eisenhardt, 'Agency Theory: An Assessment and Review' (1989) 14(1) *Academy of Management Review* 57.

37 See eg, Roberta Romano, 'After the Revolution in Corporate Law' (2005) 55(3) *Journal of Legal Education* 342.

dispute.[38] Judges decide cases based on their interpretations of legal materials – statutes, and records of the common law and equity – not a particular economic theory. A director who follows contract theory and acts as the agent of particular shareholders breaks the law and may face the impact of reality.

3.2.4 Real entity

Statute law deems companies to be entities separate from their shareholders.[39] Therefore, a theory that conceptualises a discrete corporate existence has an obvious attraction since, unlike contract theory, it is consistent with the law. It is also appealing because it opens the door to a corporate purpose beyond the presumption of short-term maximisation of shareholder wealth either through distributions or capital growth. Despite its usefulness in certain regards, real theory tends to describe organisational behaviour.

Organisations, despite lacking physical form, may, so real entity proponents argue, be 'real in a social sense' since 'they affect human behaviour and so are real in their consequences'.[40] But a phenomenon does not need to be 'real' in order to affect human behaviour or to have observable consequences. A rumour, for example, has no concrete form, arguably no existence as such, but may alter behaviour and have social consequences. Besides, the observations on effects are not specific to bodies corporate; they also apply to other business organisations, such as large professional partnerships, and other human associations, including university faculties, criminal gangs and army regiments. Social consequences are not, therefore, dependent on legal personality. Under the cover of all-encompassing brands, multinational business organisations typically comprise various business vehicles, some of which have juristic personality and others do not. Constituent vehicles often include corporations (limited and unlimited liability), partnerships (general and limited) and trusts (common law and civil law foundations). Real entity theory does not, therefore, present a theory of the company as an entity. Like team production theory,[41] it is essentially an exercise in empirical observation of what actually happens in business organisations. My argument here may appear disparaging but real entity and team production observations are precisely what we need in order to understand what businesses, some of which happen to be incorporated, do and how they should be regulated.

Companies may be understood 'as autonomous actors with processes that shape and are shaped by natural actors'.[42] Again this observation applies

38 See Oliver Wendell Holmes, 'The Path of the Law' (1897) 10 *Harvard Law Review* 457, 461.

39 See eg, *Companies Act 1993* (NZ) s 15.

40 See Eva Micheler, *Company Law: A Real Entity Theory* (Oxford University Press, 2017) 21.

41 See generally, Blair and Stout (n 5).

42 See Micheler (n 40) 31.

equally to other organisations but not all corporations. An organisation needs a critical mass of human associates before individuality may be subsumed within the collective. A large unincorporated partnership may have such critical mass but a corporation sole or a one-person company does not. The behaviour of a director-shareholder of a one-person company may be distorted by the protections offered by separate corporate personality and limited liability,[43] but that moral hazard is not a manifestation of the herd instinct in terms of which individual autonomy is lost within the group.[44]

Company regulation, like the oversight of all social arrangements, is essentially about regulating the conduct of people. '[I]ndividual agency plays a role in company law', and 'those designing legal interventions need to be aware of both human agency and also the potential toxicity of social structure'.[45] This is a critical insight. We need to look through the legal construct of the company to understand the behaviour of individuals in a group situation and the collective pressures that may lead organisational insiders to act against the interests of the broad political community. To reiterate, that necessity is not a matter of the law deeming companies to be legal entities but rather a recognition of herd behaviour. The disciplines of sociology, psychology and organisational behaviour could equally and adequately analyse the herd instinct and other group phenomena without claiming the company is a 'real' thing.

From an organisational behaviour perspective,[46] what matters is the possibility of belonginess to a group that transcends autonomous individuality, not the legal existence of the corporation. Although it is plausible to portray the (public) company as a managed pool of capital,[47] from an organisational perspective, the company is better conceived as just one type of human group and a potential locus of de-individualisation.

3.3 The company untheorised

What does it mean to say a company is an *entity*?

As a preliminary point, it is preferable for a statutory text to identify a body corporate as an entity, rather than a legal 'person', since the latter identifier may lead to confusion with natural persons and an anthropomorphism

43 See generally, Kahn-Freund (n 19).

44 See Gillian Swanson, 'Collectivity, Human Fulfilment and the "Force of Life": Wilfred Trotter's Concept of the Herd Instinct in Early 20th-Century Britain' (2014) 27(1) *History of the Human Sciences* 21.

45 See Micheler (n 40) 31.

46 See Michael B Metzger and Dan R Dalton, 'Seeing the Elephant: An Organizational Perspective on Corporate Moral Agency' (1996) 33(4) *American Business Law Journal* 489.

47 See eg, Susan Watson, 'The Corporate Legal Entity as a Fund' (2018) 6 *Journal of Business Law* 467.

that even the most preeminent of jurists may succumb to.[48] Since it is far from obvious what the law means when it declares a company to be an 'entity' separate from its shareholders,[49] it is understandable that economists should ignore separate corporate existence. To add to the confusion for the non-lawyer, the law also refers to the members of a partnership collectively as 'the firm',[50] which may falsely imply an entity beyond the partnership association. When economists refer to a 'firm', they typically denote a business organisation, whether that is a corporation, a partnership or any other business form.

Generally, an entity is '[s]omething that has a real existence';[51] it is 'what exists', 'a thing'.[52] How does a company exist? An attractive approach to the company as an entity that exists is to portray it as an 'enterprise'. But, since the general understanding of an enterprise is '[a] commercial or industrial undertaking; a firm, a company, a business',[53] it becomes an exercise in tautology – a company is an enterprise which is a company.

Without seeking to add to the superfluity of corporate law theories, it is submitted that companies possess the following characteristics. They are:

- Created by human agents following specific rules;[54]
- Abstract objects with no concrete form and have no existence before incorporation;[55]
- Legal actors but only through the acts of human agents;
- Betokened by concrete objects, such as branded products, constitutions, letterheads, logos;[56]
- Experienced by people; and
- Instruments for corporate actors to impact on individuals, society and the environment.[57]

48 See eg, Lord Denning's 'brain and nerve centre' and 'hands' metaphor employed in *HL Bolton (Engineering) Co Ltd v TJ Graham & Sons Ltd* [1957] 1 QB 159, 172.

49 See eg, *Companies Act 1993* (NZ) s 15.

50 See eg, *Partnership Law Act 2019* (NZ) s 10.

51 See *Oxford English Dictionary* (online).

52 See A Pablo Iannone, *Dictionary of World Philosophy* (Routledge, online ed, 2001).

53 See *Oxford English Dictionary* (online).

54 Cf *Meridian Global* (n 4) 11–12 where Lord Hoffmann characterised the company as a set of particular rules that must be interpreted within the context of the greater normative scheme of the law. Given the uncertainty about what the law means by an entity in relation to a company, it is plausible that a certain set of rules should identify a particular company.

55 Cf a work of art. The expression of a concept in the mind of the artist is an abstract object; the artefact is a concrete object that to some or other extent, depending on the skill of the artist or their amanuenses, evidences the abstract object. For a full discussion, see Jonathan Barrett, 'Copying Artistic Works: Copyright, Aesthetics, and Artistic Practice' in Jani McCutcheon and Fiona McGaughey (eds), *Research Handbook on Art and Law* (Edward Elgar, 2020) 59.

56 From a perspective of intellectual property, logos, which are typically trade mark protected, are also abstract objects but are expressed in a concrete form. A company is an abstract object that has no concrete form.

57 For a full explanation of this argument, see Jonathan Barrett, 'Metaphysics and the Corporation' (2020) 35(3) *Australian Journal of Corporate Law* 305.

Nevertheless, from a pragmatic perspective, we have no need to engage with the ontology of the company or express support for any particular theory. Controllers of and stakeholders in companies need to know the legal consequences of their actions and behaviours. Shareholders, for example, need to understand when dividends might be declared. Employees need to know their rights on insolvency, and unsecured creditors should be able to gauge in principle when directors may be held personally liable for the debts of the company. The benefits of seeking to explain these day-to-day concerns in terms of theory are elusive. Rather we should investigate ways of structuring company law and regulation that are effective and produce optimal social and economic benefits. This goal is not compatible with disciplinary silos or strong demarcations between legal and functional capacities.

3.4 Neo-concession

I have discounted real entity, team production and enterprise models as implausible or unnecessary theories of the company *as a legal person*. Nevertheless, they provide invaluable insights into corporations as businesses and organisations. Indeed, to understand commercial companies, we need to consider them through the lenses of functional and organisational capacities, as well as their legal capacities. For directors of companies, super-statutes governing employment, occupational health and safety, consumer protection, competition law and so forth are crucial considerations from an operational perspective,[58] rather than hypothetical duties owed to an abstract object.

Neo-concession is not a rival theory of the corporation, rather it is an exercise in identifying the context in which the State permits certain business arrangements to be incorporated as companies. Beyond a vague concept of public interest, we need to consider the fullest context of the legal and ethical ecosphere of the human rights State. The United Nations (UN) human rights instruments and explanatory commentaries tell us in detail how human rights should be protected, promoted and respected.

It would be disingenuous to claim that the neo-concession approach is ideologically neutral since the human rights moral megalogue has been identified as the principal characteristic of human rights States. The fundamental human rights tenets of respect for individual dignity, on the one hand, and social interdependence, on the other hand, exclude extreme forms of communitarianism and libertarianism. But, within these outer margins, the broadest range of ideological stances can affirm universal human rights. Nevertheless, the fullest realisation of universal human rights is an inherently progressive project and so it would be incongruous to adopt a laissez-faire approach to regulation of the company in that context.

58 On the proposal of super-statutes, see William N Eskridge Jr and John Ferejohn, 'Super-Statutes' (2001) 50(5) *Duke Law Journal* 1215.

3.5 Concluding comments

A model of the corporation should have resonance in the context in which it is proposed. The resurrection of the *corpus mysticum* in the commercially laissez-faire but religiously fervent late nineteenth-century United States gained traction because it justified free association without permission of the State.[59] In an era of dominant free market liberalism, in which the State was expected to play an ancillary role to business, economics-driven contractual theories made sense. Today, we appear to be more suspicious of unbridled capitalism and the assumption that the sole function of the business corporation is to maximise short-term shareholder wealth. In academic and popular discourse, the idea of stakeholders, rather than the body of shareholders, being synonymous with the company, and therefore the concern of directors, has taken hold.[60]

Since contemporary companies have few if any restraints on their legal capacity, functional capacity is likely to be of far more significant concern for directors. The business operations a registered company may conduct are subject to a plethora of laws and regulations, and, for many activities, licensing. These concerns have little connection to corporate theory but should be pressing issues for corporate actors.

While we may be wary of voluntary and self-reported corporate social responsibility claims,[61] many companies are choosing to expose themselves to non-governmental organisation and consumer scrutiny by joining the UN Global Compact.[62] Others have undergone B-Corp certification.[63] The 'protect, respect and remedy' imperatives of the UN Guiding Principles on Business and Human Rights are being adopted as norms, rather than recommendations.[64] Generally, the concept of social licence is increasingly asserted,[65]

59 See generally, Porterfield (n 15).

60 See eg, 'Britain needs business at its best', *Better Business Act* (Web Page, 2024) <https://betterbusinessact.org/>.

61 See eg, Honglei Mu and Youngchan Lee, 'Greenwashing in Corporate Social Responsibility: A Dual-Faceted Analysis of Its Impact on Employee Trust and Identification' (2023) 15(22) *Sustainability* 15693.

62 See 'Our participants', *United Nations Global Compact* (Web Page, 2024) <https://unglobalcompact.org/what-is-gc/participants>.

63 See 'About B Corp certification', *B Lab* (Web Page, 2024) <https://www.bcorporation.net/en-us/certification/>.

64 See eg, Claire Methven O'Brien and Roberto Caranta, *Due Diligence in EU Institutions' Own-Account Procurement: Rules and Practices* (Policy Department for Budgetary Affairs, European Parliament, 2024).

65 See eg, Karin Buhmann, 'Public Regulator and CSR: The "Social Licence to Operate" in Recent United Nations Instruments of Business and Human Rights and the Juridification of CSR' (2016) 136(4) *Journal of Business Ethics* 699.

especially when a business operation may cause environmental damage.[66] A neo-concession approach to company law and regulation plausibly speaks to this developing context.

A leading Australian jurist has argued:

> we should be looking at company law, with the benefit of empirical data concerning the reality of the economy and society in which corporations in Australia today must operate. Any study of company law which ignores globalisation, institutional dominance of investment funds, the impact of technology and down-sizing of employment and the growth of privatisation of formerly governmental corporation is bound to come up with artificial and ineffective responses.[67]

This counsel to avoid a decontextualised consideration of company law – as a unique focus on legal capacity, rather than business functions – remains persuasive.

66 See eg, P Edwards and S Trafford, 'Social Licence in New Zealand – What Is It?' (2016) 46 (3-4) *Journal of the Royal Society of New Zealand* 165. Increasingly, the interests of Indigenous Peoples are becoming a critical issue for social licences. See eg, *Trans-Tasman Resources Limited v Taranaki-Whanganui Conservation Board & Others* [2021] NZSC 127 on Māori and others' objections to ecologically destructive extraction of iron sands.

67 See Michael Kirby, 'Australian Corporations Law and Global Forces' (1997) 2(1) *Flinders Journal of Law Reform* 41, 51.

4 Law and legislative considerateness

4.1 Introduction

This chapter selectively considers three issues relating to companies legislation – legislative considerateness, directors' duties, including the relationship with shareholders and other stakeholders, and piercing the corporate veil. Statutory provisions should be consistent with the contemporary business and human rights context of neo-concession.[1] In this regard, the first stated purpose of the *Companies Act 2008* (South Africa) is to 'promote compliance with the Bill of Rights as provided for in the Constitution, in the application of company law'.[2] To reiterate, the South African bill of rights is based on the *Universal Declaration of Human Rights* (UDHR) and includes guarantees of cultural, economic, environmental and social rights, as well as civil and political rights. It also applies in horizontal and vertical directions. This legislation, therefore, provides a template for companies law that puts human rights in the forefront of consideration.

4.1.1 Legislative considerateness

Legislative considerateness requires lawmakers to ensure that statutes meet the needs of competent and cooperative citizens and facilitate their compliance obligations. (Chapter 5 discusses regulatory considerateness.) Legislative considerateness is particularly relevant to small and medium enterprises (SMEs). Most companies, in number but not economic power, are SMEs.[3] Many SMEs are likely to be incorporated partnerships in substance and so do not correspond with traditional conceptions of the corporation and models that tend to inform incorporating statutes.[4]

1 See in particular, 'Guiding Principles on Business and Human Rights: Implementing the United Nations "Protect, Respect and Remedy" Framework', *Office of the High Commission for Human Reports* (Report, 2011) <https://www.ohchr.org/sites/default/files/documents/publications/guidingprinciplesbusinesshr_en.pdf>.

2 See *Companies Act 2008* (South Africa) s 7(a).

3 See eg, Lynn Taylor, 'Corporate Enterprises' in Susan Watson and Lynn Taylor (eds), *Corporate Law in New Zealand* (Thomson Reuters, 2018) 97, 99–100.

4 See ibid.

DOI: 10.4324/9781003509066-4

4.1.2 Directors' duties

Directors' duties, in particular the fundamental duty of loyalty, originated in trust law. Indeed, in Canada before 1855, the controllers of companies were statutorily identified as 'trustees'.[5] But directors are not trustees and, whereas trustees own the trust corpus, the corporate entity owns its assets.[6] Consequently, trust law can only be applied analogously to company directors. Does path dependency on the rules of equity meet the needs of the modern corporation? This chapter argues for a reassessment of the role of directors and the duties they owe. Focus should shift from an inquiry about to whom duties are owed to a statement of principles on the behaviour expected of directors that meets the needs of close and indirect stakeholders. How 'the shareholder' is imagined by the lawmaker is an important consideration here.

4.1.3 Piercing the corporate veil

A corollary of the grant of legal personality is the State's right to suspend a company's separate existence, ignore that existence or to remove a company from the register of companies under appropriate circumstances. Specific statutory provisions may apply, for example pooling of group assets on insolvency, but it is generally left to the courts to decide on an ad hoc and often incoherent basis whether the corporate veil may be lifted or pierced.[7] I raise the question for debate whether companies Acts should include a general power to set aside corporate personality akin to a general anti-avoidance rule which is commonly included in tax legislation.[8]

4.2 Legislative considerateness

This section outlines general principles that should apply to all statutes, including corporation Acts.

4.2.1 General principles

Generally, statutes should be proportionate,[9] reasonable, transparent and effective. In addition to being consistent with human rights, legislation should adhere

5 See EE Palmer, 'Directors' Powers and Duties' in Jacob S Ziegel (ed), *Canadian Company Law* (Butterworths, 1967) 365, 366.

6 See ibid 367.

7 See Lord Sumption's analysis in *Prest v Petrodel Resources Ltd* [2013] UKSC 34.

8 See eg, Susi Baerentzen, *The Effectiveness of General Anti-Avoidance Rules: Their Limits, Challenges and Potential in EU and International Tax Law* (IBFD, 2022).

9 See eg, Aharon Barak, 'Proportional Effect: The Israeli Experience' (2007) 57(2) *University of Toronto Law Journal* 369; Richard Stacey, 'Proportionality Analysis by the South African Constitutional Court' in Mordechai Kremnitzer, Talya Steiner and Andrej Lang (eds), *Proportionality in*

to 'distinct rules of legal excellence' or principles defining 'the internal morality of law'.[10] Statutes should manifest generality; prospective operation; intelligibility and clarity; avoidance of contradictions and impossible demands; constancy through time; and congruence between official action and publication.[11]

Predictability lies at the root of the law.[12] For legislation, the possibility of prediction starts with the ability to understand the text. Yet the power to interpret and make decisions regarding statutes tends to vest in a relatively small number of people, typically legal practitioners.

> Although the law is reason, reason alone will not give mastery of it … Thus, obviously, actual knowledge of law is denied to the community. This knowledge is necessarily – by its nature – the monopoly of lawyers, who appear as the absolutely indispensable representatives of the community in stating, interpreting and applying the law.[13]

Transparent governance implies drafting of legislative texts to ensure they are readily comprehensible to everyone who must comply, rather than a coterie of specialists. Cost and ignorance may present considerable barriers to understanding the law.[14]

Provided the purpose and principles of a statute are adequately and concisely formulated, exclusionary texts may be redrafted in plain language.[15] Brevity is not, however, the primary concern. An accessible text may be lengthy because it incorporates diagrams, flowcharts, readers' notes and a list of definitions as interpretative aids. Plain language texts require considerable discipline in the formulation and communication of policy and core principles.[16]

4.2.2 Legislative considerateness and SMEs

Legislative considerateness manifests when lawmakers take proper account of the needs and capacities of the people who must comply with the law.

Action: Comparative and Empirical Perspectives on the Judicial Practice (Cambridge University Press, 2020) 193.

10 See Lon L Fuller, *The Morality of Law* (rev ed, Yale University Press, 1969) 42.

11 See ibid.

12 See Oliver Wendell Holmes, 'The Path of the Law' (1897) 10 *Harvard Law Review* 457, 461.

13 See Roger Cotterrell, *The Politics of Jurisprudence: A Critical Introduction to Legal Philosophy* (University of Pennsylvania Press, 1989) 34.

14 See Philippe Nonet, 'Legal Competence' in CM Campbell and Paul Wiles (eds), *Law and Society* (Martin Robertson, 1979) 268. Nonet observes that although the aim of the legal order is that everyone should be equal before the law, notwithstanding their power, social standing or political leverage, the administration of law does not work in a vacuum.

15 See John Avery Jones, 'Tax Law: Rules or Principles?' (1996) 17(3) *Fiscal Studies* 63.

16 See 'Legislation Guidelines' *Legislation Design and Advisory Committee* (Report, 2021) <https://www.lac.org.nz/assets/documents/LDAC-Legislation-Guidelines-2021-edition.pdf>.

SMEs, which are commonly incorporated partnerships in substance,[17] generally deserve greater legislative consideration than large companies which can afford to employ and engage expert advisors. Rather than pools of capital, de facto incorporated partnerships may be seen as pools of skill or professional knowledge, and yet are usually subject to the same rules as traditional companies.

In 1984, South Africa, recognising the critical role small businesses play in the market economy, became the first country with a UK-heritage company law system to provide legislation suitable for SMEs.[18] In terms of the *Close Corporations Act 1984* (South Africa), a close corporation (CC) is a legal entity with perpetual succession. A CC has no share capital or shareholders. The owners, who are the members of the CC, hold a membership interest, expressed as a percentage. Membership is generally restricted to natural persons, and one CC may not hold an interest in another CC. The minimum number of members is one and the maximum number of members is ten.[19]

A leading commentor observed in 2007:

> the close corporation is particularly well set to fulfil its primary object at least for the next decade, that is of meeting the reasonable needs and expectations of the typical small entrepreneur without burdening him or her with legal requirements that would not be meaningful in his circumstances, in other words of simply 'thinking small first'.[20]

Paradoxically then, from 1 May 2011, when the *Companies Act 2008* (South Africa) came into effect, no new CCs could be registered or any conversion from a company to a CC allowed. (Since CCs have perpetual existence, presumably regulatory infrastructure will need to be retained long into the future.) It appears that CCs were discontinued to streamline the differences between CCs and companies, and to make the private company a more attractive form of business enterprise. Even if the South African government has determined that the CC is unworthy of further promotion, it nevertheless provides a template that may be considered and adapted by other jurisdictions.[21]

17 See eg, Taylor (n 3) 99–100.

18 See JJ Henning, 'Close Corporations without End. Two Remarkable Decades of Simply "Thinking Small First"' (2007) 32(1) *Journal for Juridical Science* 187, 187.

19 See 'Close Corporations (CC)' *SARS* (2021) <https://www.sars.gov.za>.

20 See Henning (n 18) 192.

21 In addition to the usual distinction drawn between private (proprietary) and public companies, *Corporations Act 2001* (Cth) s 45A(2) defines a 'small proprietary company' which has reduced financial reporting obligations. New Zealand's company regulation regime is 'one size fits all' but *Companies Act 1993* (NZ) s 207K provides reduced financial reporting obligations for companies with fewer than ten shareholders.

Unlike US limited liability companies (LLCs),[22] a CC is not taxed on a flow-through basis.[23] In contrast, qualifying closely held New Zealand companies can opt for tax transparent treatment in the way of a partnership.[24] This concession indicates that tax laws may be more attuned to the substance of SME companies than companies Acts.

4.3 Directors' duties

As a fundamental principle, directors must be autonomous human beings. (Chapter 7 discusses directorial autonomy in the face of emerging technology.) As people responsible for a business – like sole proprietors, partners and trustees of business trusts – they owe numerous legal duties to their customers, employees and competitors, based on the functions their businesses perform. But unlike partners and trustees, they do not owe fiduciary duties to human beings, who may be able to protect their own interests – they owe their fundamental duty to an abstract object. Courts and theorists have sought to overcome this apparent absurdity by equating the corporate entity with shareholders or stakeholders, or by ignoring the legal proclamation that a company is a discrete entity. Given the legal existence of the corporation, a duty of directorial loyalty seems necessary, but legislation could place far greater emphasis on principles of directorial behaviour than a fiduciary owed to an abstract object.

Demanding a duty of corporate loyalty from the sole director-shareholder of a one-person company presents as legal pedantry and may be challengingly hypothetical. However, if such a director, say, usurps a corporate opportunity for their own benefit, the company's ability to pay its employees and meet its debts may be compromised. These possibilities can be addressed by behavioural principles that establish protections for employees and creditors and give them standing to sue a director who misbehaves. Does this approach ignore corporate existence? I would argue that it pragmatically recognises that corporate existence should have a narrow purpose (holding and protecting corporate property). The law should take account of who suffers loss as a lived experience. Company accounts may need to record a financial deficit, but the lives of close stakeholders may be affected in ways that impact on their ability to flourish as human beings. Shareholders should most obviously be considered but also employees and creditors, who have concluded contracts with the company in the understanding that its controllers will not deliberately jeopardise its ability to meet its contractual obligations.

22 See 'LLC filing as a corporation or partnership', *IRS* (Web Page, 2023) <https://www.irs.gov/businesses/small-businesses-self-employed/llc-filing-as-a-corporation-or-partnership>.

23 See 'Close Corporations (CC)' (n 19).

24 See *Income Tax Act 2007* (NZ) s CB 32.

Post-*Salomon*,[25] it is said that either you have a company, or you do not. Neo-classical economists prefer the latter option and ignore the inconvenient fact of the law but, under current law, directors and their advisors need to understand what constitutes the best interests of the company.

Since the doctrine of shareholder primacy conflates the interests of the company with those of the general body of shareholders, it constitutes an exercise in perceptually piercing the veil. Equating the company's interests with those of its broader stakeholders also suggests veil piercing. Only models which consider the company itself as a long-term enterprise seem loyal to the statutory obligation.[26] For example a director who usurps a corporate opportunity or deliberately incurs debts the company cannot pay clearly acts against the long-term interests of the enterprise and breaches their duties to the company.

An enterprise or sustainable entity approach is not anti-shareholder since a business which cannot attract or retain capital is not sustainable in the long term. Furthermore, a business that exploits its employees or bilks its creditors is unlikely to survive. And, of course, a business that fails to pay its taxes or trashes the environment is unlikely to survive into the long term. The word 'business' is used here deliberately since, while corporate statutory provisions are specific to companies, sustainability concerns apply to any sizeable enterprise.

To reiterate, rather than trying to interpret duties owed to an abstract object, directors need principles to guide them in performing their functions in context. Irish legislation does this to some extent. *Companies Act 2014* (Ireland) s 224(1) (CA 2014) provides:

> The matters to which the directors of a company are to have regard in the performance of their functions shall include the interests of the company's employees in general, as well as the interests of its members.

In providing guidance on the performance of directorial functions, this provision identifies two close stakeholders of the company (and significantly places employees before members in the statutory text). But the text then reasserts the traditional and overriding duty of loyalty:

> Accordingly, the duty imposed by this section on the directors shall be owed by them to the company (and the company alone) and shall be enforceable in the same way as any other fiduciary duty owed to a company by its directors.

25 See *Salomon v A Salomon & Co Ltd* [1896] UKHL 1.

26 See eg, Andrew Keay, *The Corporate Objective* (Edward Elgar, 2011); Susan M Watson, 'The Corporate Legal Entity as a Fund' (2018) 6 *Journal of Business Law* 467. Enterprise conceptions of the company are generally traced to E Merrick Dodd Jr, 'For Whom Are Corporate Managers Trustees?' (1932) 45(7) *Harvard Law Review* 1145.

Following a European Directive,[27] CA 2014 s 224A provides:

> A director of a company who believes, or who has reasonable cause to believe, that the company is, or is likely to be, unable to pay its debts (within the meaning of section 509(3)), shall have regard to –
>
> (a) the interests of the creditors,
> (b) the need to take steps to avoid insolvency, and
> (c) the need to avoid deliberate or grossly negligent conduct that threatens the viability of the business of the company.
>
> The duty imposed by this section on a director shall be owed by them to the company (and the company alone) and shall be enforceable in the same way as any other fiduciary duty owed to a company by its directors.

Furthermore, a paragraph (i) was added to section 228(1) (fiduciary duties) and states:

> In addition to the duties under section 224A (directors to have regard to certain matters where company is, or is likely to be, unable to pay its debts), [a director of a company shall] have regard to the interests of its creditors where the directors become aware of the company's insolvency.

CA 2014 contemplates a small number of stakeholders who are close to the company. It provides a plausible third way between shareholder primacy and open-ended stakeholder claims for directorial consideration. It is not, however, beyond critique. The phrase 'who believes, or who has reasonable cause to believe' unhelpfully blurs the distinction between subjective and objective tests, although it may be borne in mind that both subjectivity and objectivity as criteria are changeable social constructs.

So how could we make the Irish template more useful still?

Members of society can expect a reasonable ability on the part of directors. (Chapter 5 discusses the role the regulator can play in promoting competence.) We would not allow, say, a person who operates a stop-go sign to hide behind subjective honesty in the performance of their duties and so why should we allow a company director that protection?

I therefore propose for discussion the following basic directorial principles, which should be supplemented by best practice guidelines negotiated by the widest range of interested persons.

27 Following the European Union (Preventive Restructuring) Regulations 2022 (which gives effect to Directive (EU) 2019/1023 of the European Parliament and of the Council of 20 June 2019 on preventive restructuring frameworks, on discharge of debt and disqualifications, and on measures to increase the efficiency of procedures concerning restructuring, insolvency, and discharge of debt, and amending Directive (EU) 2017/1132). The Directive was given domestic force in Ireland by the European Union (Preventive Restructuring) Regulations 2022 SI No 380 of 2022.

In controlling the company as a sustainable entity in accordance with the law and its constitution, a director must:

- Act honestly, reasonably, and prudently; and
- Consider the interests of employees, shareholders, and creditors.

A director may consider any other matter which might reasonably affect the sustainability of the company.

4.3.1 Shareholders

Shareholders are not the only corporate stakeholders but, under the UK-heritage model,[28] other than directors, they comprise the only group of stakeholders that has some say in the running of a company. Generally, shareholders in general meeting can appoint and remove directors, alter the constitution, approve certain material transactions and provide some oversight of the directors. In practice, many shareholders in widely held companies are passive investors. Conversely, large institutional investors can exert a disproportionate control over a widely held company through a minority shareholding. As well as having a statutorily recognised role, shareholders are the focus of considerable academic and legal attention.

Before *Salomon*, characterisation of a company as an association of investors remained plausible; after that decision, the idea of the company as an entity was ostensibly perfected, even if its meaning remains uncertain. Nevertheless, while the interests of the company were no longer equated with the shareholders in general meeting, they continued to be linked to an expanded version of the shareholder – the 'general body of shareholders', which may include future shareholders.[29] This development may have allowed directors to adopt a more expansive view of the corporate purpose, but it also required a degree of conceptualisation and speculation. Current shareholders can make their interests clear but, since directors cannot know the interests of future shareholders, who may not yet have been born,[30] they are likely to assume the lowest common denominator of wealth maximisation.

28 Cf the German Codetermination Act on worker board representation. See eg, Stefan Retry, 'Mandatory Worker Representation on the Board and Its Effect on Shareholder Wealth' (2018) 47(1) *Financial Management* 25.

29 Cf the beneficiaries of an intergenerational trust. But a trust deed is likely to specify the expectations of each generation of beneficiaries, eg, to usufructuary income or to capital.

30 Marketers and media often seek to distinguish the interests and motivations of different generations. See eg, Deep Patel, '8 Ways Generation Z Will Differ from Millennials in the Workplace', *Forbes* (online, 21 September 2017) <https://www.forbes.com/sites/deeppatel/2017/09/21/8-ways-generation-z-will-differ-from-millennials-in-the-workplace/?sh=2e6e8d7e76e5>.

Since the 1980s, shareholder primacy and stakeholder theories have dominated debate on the role of public corporations.[31]

Contractarians generally have fostered shareholder primacy and see it as the focal point of their view of the public company. The theory is predicated on the basis of a promise made by directors to shareholders that they will maximise the wealth of the shareholders. It has also been said in this context by some that, as shareholders are the owners of the company, those who manage the company should do so for the benefit of the shareholders.[32]

Writing in 2005 to celebrate the 'end of history' hegemony of economic theory in law and 'the major breakthroughs in modern finance', which would soon contribute to the Global Financial Crisis, a proponent of economics in corporate law observed:

> In the 1980s, corporate legal scholarship and practice were completely transformed in response to intellectual currents in finance and economics and new transactional developments which called for comprehensive legal innovation.[33]

The archetype of the wealth maximising shareholder is an ideologically informed construct that ignores normal human motivations and behaviour. Most of us care if workers face exploitation or the environment is degraded. Why should we put those concerns aside when we invest? Institutional investors, such as pension funds, adopt long-term perspectives and are the intermediaries for the investments of people, such as nurses, teachers and public servants, who often hold strong views about social justice. The Norwegian sovereign wealth fund is a notable activist in its shareholdings.[34] Furthermore, the predominant investment houses that manage trillions of dollars of shareholdings have committed to the UN Principles of Responsible Investment (PRI).[35] Corporate signatories to PRI include BlackRock (US$10 trillion assets under management), Vanguard (US$8 trillion assets under management) and State Street (US$4 trillion assets under management).[36] These are the world's largest shareholders and have committed to the following. We will:

31 See eg, Robert J Rhee, 'A Legal Theory of Shareholder Primacy' (2018) 102 *Minnesota Law Review* 1951.

32 See Andrew Keay, 'Ascertaining the Corporate Objective: An Entity Maximisation and Sustainability Model' (2008) 71(5) *Modern Law Review* 663, 667 (references omitted).

33 See Roberta Romano, 'After the Revolution in Corporate Law' (2005) 55(3) *Journal of Legal Education* 342, 359.

34 See 'Responsible investment', *Norges Bank Investment Management* (Web Page) <https://www.nbim.no/en/responsible-investment/>.

35 See *A Sustainable Finance Policy Engagement Handbook* (UNPRI, 28 November 2022).

36 See Farhad Manjoo, 'What BlackRock, Vanguard and State Street Are Doing to the Economy', *The New York Times* (online, 12 May 2022) <https://www.nytimes.com/2022/05/12/opinion/vanguard-power-blackrock-state-street.html>. I do not argue that these huge holdings are beneficial for the world economy or that these firms are ethically motivated.

1. Incorporate environmental, social and governance (ESG) issues into investment analysis and decision-making processes.
2. Be active owners and incorporate ESG issues into our ownership policies and practices.
3. Seek appropriate disclosure on ESG issues by the entities in which we invest.
4. Promote acceptance and implementation of the Principles within the investment industry.
5. Work together to enhance our effectiveness in implementing the Principles.
6. Each report on our activities and progress towards implementing the Principles.

While the Blair-led Labour government in the United Kingdom was noted for its 'Third Way' policies that seemed to satisfy neither conservatives nor progressives,[37] the introduction of *Companies Act 2006* (UK) s 172 represented a creative attempt to admit the possibility of an 'enlightened shareholder', who cares about more than short-term financial returns.[38] Section 172 provides:

> (1) A director of a company must act in the way he considers, in good faith, would be most likely to promote the success of the company for the benefit of its members as a whole, and in doing so have regard (amongst other matters) to—
> (a) the likely consequences of any decision in the long term,
> (b) the interests of the company's employees,
> (c) the need to foster the company's business relationships with suppliers, customers and others,
> (d) the impact of the company's operations on the community and the environment,
> (e) the desirability of the company maintaining a reputation for high standards of business conduct, and
> (f) the need to act fairly as between members of the company.

The text implies a subjective test, which should, at first face, protect the director from claims that a reasonable director would have decided differently. It also means that, say, a dyed-in-the-wool believer in the profit-maximising

37 See Andrew Leigh, 'The Rise and Fall of the Third Way' (Mar-Apr 2003) 75(2) *Australian Quarterly* 10, 14.

38 See eg, Andrew Keay, 'Tackling the Issue of the Corporate Objective: An Analysis of the United Kingdom's "Enlightened Shareholder Value Approach"' (2007) 29(4) *Sydney Law Review* 577; Virginia Harper Ho, '"Enlightened Shareholder Value": Corporate Governance Beyond the Shareholder-Stakeholder Divide' (2010) 36(1) *Journal of Corporation Law* 59; Richard Williams, 'Enlightened Shareholder Value in UK Company Law' (2012) 35(1) *UNSW Law Journal* 360.

shareholder could have regard to the listed and other matters but still aim for short-term profits. Nevertheless, the enlightened shareholder presents a more plausible archetype of the human investor than the 'Econ',[39] which informs contractarian conceptions.

If directors can rely on general behavioural principles when making decisions about sustaining the enterprise, the need to conceptualise 'the shareholder' becomes mostly redundant. We can assume most directors behave as honest, reasonable and prudent businesspeople, who recognise their situation in a particular political community, and this appears to provide an acceptable behavioural benchmark. It is, then, unnecessary to construct an archetype of the shareholder. Nevertheless, for the purposes of this study, all corporate actors are assumed to be competent and cooperative citizens of the human rights State.

4.4 General anti-abuse provision

South Africa has extended the usual oppression or prejudice action to include abuse of the separate juristic personality of a company.[40] *Companies Act 2008* s 163(4) provides:

> Whenever a court, on application by an interested person … finds that the incorporation of, or any act by or on behalf of, or any use of, that company constitutes an unconscionable abuse of the juristic personality of the company as a separate entity, the court may declare that the company is to be deemed not to be a juristic person in respect of such rights.

The Act does not define 'unconscionable abuse' or 'interested person', although it seems the latter term is not restricted to aggrieved shareholders.[41] The provision does not represent a code and may indeed be narrower in scope than the common law which may permit piercing of the veil, albeit in highly proscribed circumstances, in the event of fraud, evasion of a legal obligation or on public policy grounds.[42] Nevertheless, it expressly imports the idea into statute that incorporation is a concession that may be rescinded.

39 For a distinction drawn between 'Humans' (*Homo sapiens*) who behave like people and 'Econs' (*Homo economicus*) who are rational (in a neo-classical economics perspective) wealth maximisers, see Richard H Thaler and Cass R Sunstein, *Nudge: Improving Decisions about Health, Wealth and Happiness* (Penguin Books, 2009) 6–8.

40 See *Companies Act 2008* (South Africa) s 163. See also *Close Corporations Act 1984* (South Africa) s 65.

41 For a discussion of the provision, see Rehana Cassim, 'Piercing the corporate veil "Unconscionable abuse" under the Companies Act 71 of 2008' *De Rebus* (online, 1 August 2012) <https://www.derebus.org.za/piercing-corporate-veil-unconscionable-abuse-companies-act-71-2008/>.

42 See *Prest* (n 7) [34].

Should an abuse of legal personality provision be generally adopted?

The grounds for piercing the corporate veil are analogous to tax evasion, that is, an exercise in dishonest concealment. It might be possible to craft an abuse of corporate form provision closer in nature to tax avoidance. Avoidance is a matter of legally arranging one's affairs in a way that delivers a benefit that the legislator did not intend, such as a reduction or deferral of tax obligations. (Tax mitigation is taking advantage of benefit the legislator intended.) An element of dishonesty is not required for a scheme of avoidance. Tax statutes generally include specific anti-avoidance provisions and a general anti-avoidance rule (GAAR). Furthermore, the Organisation for Economic Co-operation and Development/G20 Base Erosion Profit Shifting (BEPS) project attempts to harness international cooperation to counter aggressive tax avoidance on the part of multi-national corporations. Two of the 15 planned BEPS actions relate directly to companies.[43]

While a general abuse provision akin to GAAR deserves policy consideration, a key problem of importing tax rules into the corporate context is that a degree of 'avoidance' or moral hazard appears to be inherent in the principles of separate legal personality and limited shareholder liability. A general abuse provision would bring uncertainty to the business sphere in which legal certainty assists planning. And so, a better approach may be to bring more certainty to piercing the veil by explaining when a court may set aside legal personality. A list could not be exhaustive but using the corporate form to abuse human rights should be the first ground.

4.5 Concluding comments

From necessity, this chapter has been highly selective. In particular, the role of directors in relation to the company attracts significant academic and judicial attention. Adhering to the pragmatism that underpins this study, to the extent possible, I have rejected conceptualisations of the shareholder and have sought to focus on an obligation for a director to behave as an honest, reasonable and prudent businessperson. While recognising that this model also entails a legal construct, it is hoped that a clear, principle-level enunciation of expectation of directors' behaviour, augmented by best practice guidelines, would remove the difficulties presented by current expressions of duties. It would also take attention away from trust law, permitting a focus on business practice.

43 See 'BEPS actions', *OECD* (Web Page) <https://www.oecd.org/tax/beps/beps-actions/>.

5 The role of the corporate regulator

5.1 Introduction

Chapter 4 focused on company statutes and legislative considerateness. In this chapter the focus of investigation shifts to how regulation supplements those statutes. Consideration is also given to the practices of the corporate regulator, including just administrative action and regulatory considerateness.

In the past two decades, regulation as a subject for academic study has stepped out from the shadow of legal analysis.[1] The particular regulatory field considered here is the registration and ongoing oversight of companies.[2] This focus excludes examination of the 'Twin Peaks' governance of offers of investments to the public and institutional financial soundness.[3] Rather the aim is to investigate the role of the regulator as intermediary between the legislative text, which permits initial and continuing incorporation, and the people who must comply with it or otherwise have an interest in the relevant law.

1 See eg, Bronwen Morgan and Karen Yeung, *An Introduction to Law and Regulation: Text and Materials* (Cambridge University Press, 2007); Robert Baldwin, Martin Cave and Martin Lodge (eds), *The Oxford Handbook of Regulation* (Oxford University Press, 2010); Peter Drahos (ed), *Regulatory Theory: Foundations and Applications* (ANU Press, 2017); Iris H-Y Chiu, 'An Institutional Theory of Corporate Regulation' (2018) 71(1) *Current Legal Problems* 279; 'Regulatory policy by country', *OECD* (Web Page) <https://www.oecd.org/gov/regulatory-policy/by-country.htm>.

2 'In this era, more of the governance that shapes the daily lives of most citizens is corporate governance than state governance. The corporatization of the world is both a product of regulation and the key driver of regulatory growth, indeed of state growth more generally'. See John Braithwaite, 'The Regulatory State?' in R Goodin (ed), *The Oxford Handbook of Political Science* (Oxford University Press, 2009) 407, 408.

3 See Andrew Godwin, Steve Kourabas and Ian Ramsay, 'Twin Peaks and Financial Regulation' (2016) 49(3) *International Lawyer* 273. The Australian Securities & Investment Commission performs the roles of both the registrar of companies and financial markets regulator.

DOI: 10.4324/9781003509066-5

5.1.1 General principles

The regulator's behaviour must, at least, be consistent with the rule of law,[4] which incorporates human rights principles,[5] proportionality, reasonableness, transparency and procedural fairness.[6] Regulation should be suited for the needs of human actors and based on mutual trust between the regulator and those regulated.[7] While the regulator must allocate scarce resources optimally, they 'should see costs and benefits not as arithmetic abstractions, but as efforts to capture qualitatively diverse goods and to promote sensible trade-offs among them'.[8] Since the regulator is an agency of the human rights State, they 'should take account of values that are different or impossible to quantify, such as dignity and autonomy'.[9] Because regulation is ultimately about engaging with human behaviour, proper consideration should be given to how people actually behave.[10] Furthermore, 'policies and regulations need to benefit from the dispersed information of a wide variety of human beings',[11] from major corporations and their advisors to one-person companies.

The functions, powers and duties of the regulator are determined by statute.[12] The regulator typically has discretion over the registration of company names.[13] As a government agency, they are bound by the State's human rights obligations and so, for example, should not register a name which offends human dignity because it may degrade a particular group in society. If the companies' statute does not meet the needs of government or those subject to regulation, the regulator has limited capacity for making good the regulatory deficit.[14] Nevertheless, they perform a quasi-judicial role, since, at first instance, they interpret relevant law, and establish processes and practices

4 See Yseult Marique, 'The Rule of Law and Administrative Justice' in Marc Hertog (ed), *The Oxford Handbook of Administrative Justice* (Oxford University Press, 2021) 305.

5 See Tom Bingham, *The Rule of Law* (Penguin Books, 2011) 66–84.

6 Cf *Constitution of the Republic of South Africa 1996* (South Africa) s 33.

7 See Peri K Blind, 'Building Trust in Government: Linking Theory with Practice' in G Shabbir Cheema and Vesselin Popovski (eds), *Building Trust in Government: Innovations in Governance Reform in Asia* (United Nations University Press, 2010) 22.

8 See Cass R Sunstein, *Valuing Life: Humanizing the Regulatory State* (University of Chicago Press, 2014) 173–74.

9 See ibid.

10 See ibid.

11 See ibid.

12 Since the Registrar of Companies (in New Zealand and UK terminology) is likely to be a senior public servant, public service legislation will also apply to their employment.

13 For a discussion of company names, see Jonathan Barrett, 'Company Names: Challenges for the Regulator' (2023) 39(1) *Australian Journal of Corporate Law* 1.

14 Cf the powers of the Commissioner of Taxation in Australia. Revenue authorities not only interpret the law but under certain circumstances may rectify the errors and omissions of Parliament and so play a quasi-legislative role. See eg, *Taxation Administration Act 1953* (Cth) sch 1 div 370.

based on that interpretation. A person who is dissatisfied with the regulator's interpretation and consequent practice must be prepared to seek judicial review – an increasingly expensive exercise.[15]

5.1.2 Key issues

Since the principal theme of this study is corporate regulation in the context of the human rights State, which grants incorporation and has extensive human rights obligations, the first issue considered in this chapter is the institutional competence of the regulator to protect and promote human rights. While the contribution may be minimal relative to that of Parliament and the courts, it is not negligible.

The second issue is regulatory considerateness. The regulator should engage proportionately and appropriately with regulated persons. This study presumes that citizens are cooperative and competent members of society, but evidence indicates that numerous controllers of small companies need help to become competent in complying with company law, including financial reporting. Human rights are about human flourishing in all areas of life. Recalling Aristotelian virtue ethics, it is appropriate for the regulator to encourage and assist corporate actors to do what is virtuous or excellent in a particular situation.

The third issue, which is noted but not examined in detail, is international cooperation.

5.2 Institutional competence

Parliament has the unique power to enact human rights legislation, but human rights are most effectively protected and promoted when a culture in public life exists 'in which these fundamental principles are seen as key to the design and delivery of policy, legislation and public services'.[16] The corporate regulator therefore has some role to play in protecting and promoting human rights.

We expect the courts to protect our human rights and they generally do perform that function but are constitutionally and institutionally constrained. Even in countries such as Canada and South Africa, where a basic law is superior to any other law, supreme courts, which are charged with interpreting bills of rights, are acutely aware of their unelected status. The South African Constitutional Court (SACC), for example, has emphasised that it

15 An ombud service is far less expensive than judicial review but is generally underused. On the different approaches of the courts and an ombud service, see eg, Richard Kirkham and Elizabeth A O'Loughlin, 'Judicial Review and Ombuds: A Systematic Analysis' (2020) *Public Law* 680.

16 See 'Joint Committee On Human Rights – Sixth Report' (UK Parliament, 2003).

has a judicial, not a political, mandate, with a fundamental role of assessing the constitutionality of a law, not its political wisdom.[17] This deference to the elected legislature makes bold judicial action in relation to positive rights less likely, but not impossible. Since South Africa's constitution includes socio-economic and environmental rights, as well as civil and political rights, the SACC's role in actively ensuring realisation of such rights is necessarily a controversial one. Despite recognising its institutional unsuitability for practically giving effect to positive rights, the SACC has made decisions that impact on the executive's allocation of scarce resources.[18] Nevertheless, a court can only regulate ex post – 'all they can do is to apply the principles to what is brought before them by others'.[19]

Some argue that we live today not so much in a *Rechtsstaat* (state governed by the rule of law) or a disciplinary society as in a 'security state',[20] in which the 'legitimacy' of a branch of government is derived from its ability to actively perform the functions of governmentality – that is, the achievement of prosperity and welfare. In the security state, 'authority would depend on the quality of political projects, the effective performance of key functions and on the actions of welfare providing administration'.[21] A binary distinction drawn between the *Rechtsstaat* and the security state is misleading. The human rights State is both governed by the rule of law and is charged with progressively delivering cultural, economic and social rights.

Because courts cannot directly deliver welfare outcomes, from a governmentality perspective, they may lack legitimacy and, indeed, authority. Courts may preserve or redistribute an individual's existing stores of wealth in accordance with the law, but they cannot create prosperity or a sustainable environment. In short, the judiciary lacks 'political creativity'[22] and so '[r]elying too much on courts may ultimately undermine rather than affirm human rights'.[23]

I have considered the role of the judiciary and the delivery of human rights at some length because an extensive body of literature exists on judicial competence which can be used analogically to consider the broadly unexamined position of the regulator.

17 See Henk Botha, 'Freedom and Constraint in Constitutional Adjudication' (2004) 20(2) *South African Journal on Hum9an Rights* 249, 250.

18 See eg, *Government of the Republic of South Africa v Grootboom* [2000] ZACC 19; *Minister of Health v Treatment Action Campaign* [2002] ZACC 15.

19 See John Laws, 'Law and Democracy' (1995) *Public Law* 72, 93.

20 See Colin Gordon, 'Governmental Rationality: An Introduction' in G Burchell, C Gordon and P Miller (eds), *The Foucault Effect: Studies in Governmentality: With Two Lectures and an Interview with Michel Foucault* (University of Chicago Press, 1991) 1, 20.

21 See Dora Kostakopoulou, 'Floating Sovereignty: Pathology or a Necessary Means of State Evolution?' (2002) 22(1) *Oxford Journal of Legal Studies* 135, 150.

22 See Laws (n 19) 93.

23 See Janet McLean, 'Legislative Invalidation, Human Rights Protection and s 4 of the New Bill of Rights Act' (2001) 4 *New Zealand Law Review* 421, 448.

Regulators are not restricted in the way of courts to determining disputes that have already arisen. They can engage in ex ante and ex post regulation and can identify issues, and within the ambit of their statutory powers remedy them. They can also anticipate issues. This possibility of regulatory considerateness is a key concern of this chapter. Even when regulators cannot solve a mischief, they are ideally placed to enter into dialogue with government ministers and policymakers. Furthermore, regulators are not bound by the doctrinal fetters that constrain courts and can draw on qualitative and quantitative research across a range of the social sciences. Disciplines that employ quantitative methods, such as statistics, actuarial science and accounting, may play a significant role in distributive decisions about social, economic or environmental rights.

Distributive justice is an important feature of human rights. When the things to be distributed are measurable, quantitative and qualitative methods may contribute to fair and rational distributive decisions. Regulators must determine how they should allocate their scarce resources. They can employ mixed methods in their decision-making: for example, is it more equitable and efficient to allocate resources in educating honest but ignorant directors or pursuing prosecution of dishonest directors? Collation and publication of data might support human rights; for example, understanding the number of female directors of companies may help counter historical discrimination.

5.3 Regulatory considerateness

The regulator may reasonably assume that corporate actors are both cooperative and competent. Corporate actors will often meet this expectation, but we also know that many people who are corporate actors are not competent and may form companies when they do not have the requisite knowledge to operate them in accordance with the law.[24] Does the regulator owe an educative obligation to these cooperative but only potentially competent people? The proposal of regulatory considerateness indicates that they do owe such a duty. To reiterate, the realisation of human rights is about human flourishing in the society of others. It is incumbent on the human rights State to promote individual flourishing in the socially accepted areas of life in which people are active.

While more sophisticated regulatory models have been developed,[25] for the current purpose of illustrating regulatory considerateness Figure 5.1 identifies three broad categories of corporate actors:

24 See eg, Melissa Belle Isle, Brett Freudenberg and Tapan Sarker, 'The Business Tax Literacy of Australian Small Businesses' (2022) 37(1) *Australian Tax Forum* 65.

25 See generally, Ian Ayres and John Braithwaite, *Responsive Regulation: Transcending the Deregulation Debate* (Oxford University Press, 1992).

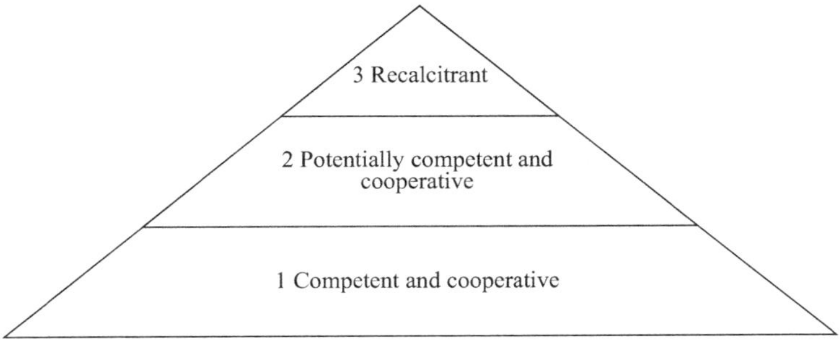

Figure 5.1 A basic model of corporate actors

1. Competent and cooperative citizens who constitute the basic archetype of a citizen;
2. Currently incompetent actors who could, with appropriate guidance, become competent citizens; and
3. Recalcitrant persons, who may be incompetent and unwilling to change or are maliciously uncooperative.

5.3.1 Competent and cooperative actors

The relationship between the regulator and competent and cooperative actors should be informed by a dialogue between equal and mutually respectful parties, who can learn from each other and progressively develop best regulatory practice. (Chapter 6 considers regulatory engagement with Indigenous Peoples.)

5.3.2 Potentially competent and cooperative actors

The relationship between the regulator and potentially competent and cooperative actors should focus on learning and should be andragogical (adult learning) or heutagogical (self-directed learning) in nature,[26] as opposed to pedagogical (children's learning), where the learner is dependent on the teacher. The regulator possesses disproportionate knowledge resources relative to many corporate actors, but the relationship should still be one of mutual respect.

The regulator should not be empowered to deny incorporation on the grounds that a corporator may appear to lack the experience or capacity to

26 See 'Pedagogy, andragogy, & heutagogy', *Center for Online Learning, Research and Service, University of Illinois Springfield* (Web Page, 2022) https://www.uis.edu/colrs/teaching-resources/foundations-good-teaching/pedagogy-andragogy-heutagogy.

comply with company law,[27] but 'speedbumps' could be introduced into the registration process. For example, a corporator who, in the case of a small or medium enterprise will most likely be a nominated director, could be nudged towards a multi-choice questionnaire akin to a provisional driving licence.[28] If they fail to answer a question correctly, they could be directed to a plain language guide to the issue, and invited to retest themselves. The first function of Ireland's Director of Corporate Enforcement is to *encourage* compliance with the *Companies Act 2014*.[29] The Corporate Enforcement Authority, which is a separate agency from the Registrar of Companies, has produced a suite of plain language guides covering various matters of interest to corporate actors.[30]

5.3.3 Recalcitrant actors

The State has a near monopoly over legitimate force. If encouragement to comply with the law made under the conditions of the human rights State is met with recalcitrance, then the regulator should be empowered to take proportionate action. Even so, we should not expect a rush to prosecution but rather a progression of responses determined by an assessment of the socio-economic risks presented by the breach.

5.4 International issues

Corporate regulators should follow and participate in international efforts to develop best practice, for example through the Organisation for Economic Co-operation and Development (OECD).[31] This section, however, focuses on an old issue – recognition of foreign companies doing business in a jurisdiction beyond their seat of registration. While this issue has been controversial for almost two centuries, it is exacerbated by aggressively permissive regulation by certain jurisdictions.[32]

27 Cf a person who may be prohibited from managing a company because of previous dishonest behaviour. See eg, *Companies Act 1993* (NZ) s 382.

28 On nudging, see generally, Richard H Thaler and Cass R Sunstein, *Nudge: Improving Decisions about Health, Wealth and Happiness* (Penguin Books, 2009).

29 See *Companies Act 2014* (Ireland) s 949(1)(a).

30 See 'Information & guidance', *CEA* (Web Page, 2024) <https://cea.gov.ie/en-ie/Publications/Information-Guidance>.

31 See 'International regulatory co-operation – transforming rulemaking to meet the global challenges of the 21st century', *OECD* (Web Page) <https://www.oecd.org/gov/regulatory-policy/irc.htm>.

32 For a fuller discussion of the relevant issues, see Jonathan Barrett, 'The Regulatory Challenges of Pseudo-foreign Corporations and Pseudo-corporations: A Neo-concession Approach' (2022) 38(1) *Australian Journal of Corporate Law* 1.

5.4.1 Recognition of out-of-jurisdiction registered companies

In *Bank of Augusta v Earle*,[33] the US Supreme Court held:

> a corporation can have no legal existence out of the boundaries of the sovereignty by which it is created. It exists only in contemplation of law and by force of the law, and where that law ceases to operate and is no longer obligatory, the corporation can have no existence. It must dwell in the place of its creation, and cannot migrate to another sovereignty.[34]

In common law countries that doctrinaire concession-based approach has long been superseded by laissez-faire recognition of any company registered by a competent authority in any jurisdiction.[35] In this scheme, consideration is not given to the possibility of pseudo-foreign corporations. For example, Australian corporators may opt to register their company in a lax regulatory jurisdiction, such as the British Virgin Islands (BVI), and then carry on business in Australia with a board of corporate directors,[36] which is not permitted under Australian law but is under BVI law. (Chapter 7 discusses regulation of pseudo-corporations, those being arrangements that may resemble traditional companies but are substantively different.) Furthermore, vehicles which are different in substance from local companies may be recognised. New Zealand, for example, recognises US limited liability companies as overseas companies, even though they may be substantively different from traditional US corporations.[37]

Rather than blithely accepting foreign incorporation, and thereby admitting the possibility of pseudo-foreign corporations, continental European jurisdictions tend to consider the real seat of management (*siège social réel*) of a corporation before granting recognition. This approach potentially requires a cumbersome investigation and adds uncertainty to cross-border arrangements. In contrast, 'the incorporation rule provides certainty and easy application',[38] but 'how big a price do we want to pay for certainty when a rule giving us

33 See *Bank of Augusta v Earle* 38 US 519 (1839) ('*Bank of Augusta*'). For a discussion of the decision, see Thomas Reed Powell, 'The Changing Law of Foreign Corporations' (1918) 33(4) *Political Science Quarterly* 549.

34 See *Bank of Augusta* (n 33) 520.

35 See JH Diephuis, 'Recognition of Foreign Companies and Bodies Corporate: The Concept of Recognition, a Short Historical Review and a Critical Analysis of the Main Provisions of the EEC Recognition Convention' (2009) 27(3) *Netherlands International Law Review* 347.

36 The *BVI Business Companies Act 2004* (BVI) s 2 refers to a director being a person, which reference appears to include legal persons. Consultancy firms advise that BVI allows a solo corporate director. See eg, 'BVI company incorporation and partnership formation', *Ogier* (Web Page, 17 January 2019) <https://www.ogier.com/publications/bvi-company-incorporation-and-partnership-formation>.

37 See 'Companies register', *New Zealand Companies Office* (Web Page, 2022) <https://companies-register.companiesoffice.govt.nz/>.

38 See Elvin R Latty, 'Pseudo-Foreign Corporations' (1955) 65(2) *Yale Law Journal* 137, 139.

certainty leads to undesirable results?'[39] 'The sensible solution ... is to stick to the certain rule until – but only until – there are strong policy reasons for doing otherwise'.[40] But those strong policy reasons may be difficult to predict.[41]

Registration or chartering shopping has become normalised in the United States where more than two-thirds of Fortune 500 companies are domiciled in Delaware,[42] and some 93% of all US initial public offerings are entities registered in that state.[43] While Delaware continues to dominate US corporate regulation, Wyoming, in particular, has sought to challenge the dominance of corporate-friendly regulation and has also earned the reputation as an onshore tax haven.[44]

> Chartering governments decide who – or what – can have the rights of a person by acting through an entity. Chartering governments also decide what information about the human actors will be available to the public, what information will be available to police and prosecutors, how quickly that information will be made available and at what expense, how quickly and easily an entity can flee a jurisdiction to avoid the jurisdiction's current or proposed regulations, and even whether a tort creditor can recover against an entity's owner. Chartering governments decide these issues *even when the effects are felt entirely outside the chartering jurisdiction*.[45]

The OECD/G20 Base Erosion Profit Shifting (BEPS) project, if fully effectuated, will combat tax avoidance by multi-national enterprises.[46] BEPS Action 2 relates to the neutralisation of hybrid mismatches, including when an entity is treated as a taxable corporation in one jurisdiction but as a tax flow-through vehicle in another jurisdiction.[47] Laxly regulated jurisdictions play a crucial

39 See ibid 140.

40 See ibid.

41 Cf how the House of Lords determined the enemy 'character' of a company, notwithstanding its incorporation in the UK, in *Daimler Co Ltd v Continental Tyre and Rubber Co (Great Britain) Ltd* [1916] UKHL 845; [1916] 2 AC 307. See also *R (Factortame Ltd) v Secretary of State for Transport* [1991] UKHL 7.

42 For a discussion of historic 'chartermongering' in the United States, see Christopher Grandy, 'New Jersey Corporate Chartermongering, 1875–1929' (1989) 49(3) *Journal of Economic History* 677.

43 See 'Annual report statistics', *Delaware Division of Corporations* (Web Page) <https://corp.delaware.gov/stats/>. Delaware also attracts foreign corporators. See eg, William J Moon, 'Delaware's Global Competitiveness' (2021) 106(4) *Iowa Law Review* 1683.

44 See eg, Debbie Cenziper and Will Fitzgibbon, 'The "Cowboy Cocktail": How Wyoming Became One of the World's Top Tax Havens', *The Washington Post* (Web Page, 20 December 2021) <https://www.washingtonpost.com/business/interactive/2021/wyoming-trusts-finance-pandora-papers/>.

45 See Lynn M LoPucki, 'Algorithmic Entities' (2018) 95 *Washington University Law Review* 887, 980 (emphasis in original).

46 See 'International collaboration to end tax avoidance', *OECD* (Web Page) <https://www.oecd.org/tax/beps/>.

47 See 'Action 2: Neutralising the effects of hybrid mismatch arrangements', *OECD* (Web Page) <https://www.oecd.org/tax/beps/beps-actions/action2/>.

role in structuring hybrid entities. They are also implicated in more traditional forms of tax avoidance.[48]

In contrast to BEPS, corporate law and regulation seems to be in thrall to free market liberalism. Facilitating egregious abuse,[49] until 2015 New Zealand did not require any director of a New Zealand-incorporated company to live in the country.[50] Today, as an alternative to a resident director, an acceptable director may live 'in an enforcement country' provided they are 'a director of a body corporate that is incorporated in that enforcement country under a law that is equivalent to' the New Zealand Act.[51] This principle of equivalent law should apply to the recognition of foreign companies.

5.5 Concluding comments

Good regulation is expensive, but the consequences of poor regulation can be massive. The leaky building syndrome which was greatly attributable to lax regulation is thought to have cost C$4 billion in British Columbia,[52] and as much as NZ$47 billion in New Zealand, roughly 20% of the country's annual gross domestic product.[53] And so an optimal balance needs to be struck between innovation-stifling state control and the 'red tape' slashing that is embraced by libertarians. I support cost-efficient and innovative regulation, such as regulatory sandboxes which permit cutting-edge businesses to work with regulators as they develop their products and models.[54] But regulatory openness to innovation and small-scale experimentation does not imply long-term competition, laxity or a rush to normalise through nominal regulation

48 See eg, Nassim Khadem, 'Multinationals Tax Dispute: Chevron Loses Appeal, Ordered to Pay about $300m to ATO', *The Sydney Morning Herald* (online, 21 April 2017) <https://www.smh.com.au/business/the-economy/chevron-loses-appeal-ordered-to-pay-more-than-300-million-in-tax-20170420-gvondk.html>.

49 See eg, Matt Nippert, 'Shell Company Barriers in Place', *Sunday-Star Times* (online, 29 June 2014) <https://www.pressreader.com/new-zealand/sunday-star-times/20140629/282329678033251>.

50 See *Companies Act 1993* (NZ) s 10(d)(i), as amended by *Companies Amendment Act 2014* (NZ) s 9.

51 See *Companies Act 1993* (NZ) s 10(d)(ii), as amended by *Regulatory Systems (Commercial Matters) Amendment Act 2017* (NZ) s 15.

52 See 'Leaky building syndrome – NZ, Canada and Australian experiences', *Lovegrove & Cotton* (Web Page, 26 September 2022) <https://lclawyers.com.au/leaky-building-syndrome-nz-canada-and-australian-experiences/>.

53 See Rob Stock, 'The "Rottenomics" of the $47 billion leaky homes market failure', *Stuff* (Web Page, 3 October 2019) <https://www.stuff.co.nz/business/116236850/the-rottenomics-of-the-47-billion-leaky-homes-market-failure>.

54 See eg, 'Hardly child's play: North Carolina joins the growing number of states with a FinTech regulatory sandbox', *The National Law Review* (Web Page, 19 October 2021) <https://www.natlawreview.com/article/hardly-child-s-play-north-carolina-joins-growing-number-states-fintech-regulatory>; Patrick Gleason, 'Regulatory sandboxes give states an edge attracting innovation and investment', *Forbes* (Web Page, 21 December 2021) <https://www.forbes.com/sites/patrickgleason/2021/12/31/regulatory-sandboxes-give-states-an-edge-attracting-innovation-and-investment/?sh=1d130cd97003>.

uncertain arrangements.[55] Ultimately, the role of the regulator is to serve the public interest, not to benefit special interest groups. In the human rights State, public interest lies in balancing the human flourishing claims of all members of the political community – corporations, especially foreign corporations, are not 'we the people'.

55 Wyoming's granting a bank charter to the cryptocurrency exchange Kraken may present as an attempt to tame the sometimes-anarchic world of cryptocurrency exchanges. See Milad Emamian, 'The cowboy state tames Bitcoin's regulatory wild west', *The Regulatory Review* (Web Page, 7 April 2021) <https://www.theregreview.org/2021/04/07/emamian-cowboy-state-tames-bitcoins-regulatory-wild-west/>. However, registration may be a matter of adding a veneer of respectability to ventures that may need more investigation before they are endorsed by the State.

6 Towards regulatory confederation

6.1 Introduction

Trade is central to a flourishing social existence.[1] In precolonial societies, trade typically evolved organically into deep and complex systems of trust and exchange.[2] Colonialism disrupted traditional Indigenous trade practices and imposed a capitalist framework which greatly obliterated customs, and marginalised local enterprise.[3] Regeneration and reconstitution of Indigenous trade in a contemporary context is a crucial element of decolonisation. Successful Indigenous businesses have community multipliers. Community wealth may be built, and local jobs generated, thereby enabling retention of local talent. Generally, the quality of community life may be improved, and group autonomy enhanced.[4] Business vehicles and regulations in postcolonial countries must meet the needs of Indigenous entrepreneurs and their communities. It is also critical to understand that Indigenous trade and enterprise is invariably linked to traditional lands and waters.

> There are few areas of human community in which tradition is more important and involves a more complex confusion of the secular and the sacred, than land. First Nations tradition and culture is tied to the land in ways that most non-First Nations cultures have long forgotten.[5]

1 See eg, Armin W Schulz, 'Tools of the Trade: The Bio-cultural Evolution of the Human Propensity to Trade' (2022) 37(8) *Biology & Philosophy* <https://doi.org/10.1007/s10539-022-09837-2>.

2 See generally, Michael Mihalicz, *Indigenous Entrepreneurship* (Pressbooks, 2022).

3 See eg, The Independent Working Group on Constitutional Transformation, 'He Whakaaro Here Whakaumu Mō Aotearoa: The Report of Matike Mai Aotearoa' (2016) 49.

4 See Stephen Cornell et al., 'Citizen Entrepreneurship: An Underutilized Development Resource' in Miriam Jorgensen (ed), *Rebuilding Native Nations: Strategies for Governance and Development* (University of Arizona Press, 2007) 197, 199–203.

5 See Michael Asch (ed), *Aboriginal and Treaty Rights in Canada: Essays on Law, Equality, and Respect for Difference* (University of British Columbia Press, 1997) cited by John Curry, Han Donker and Richard Krehbiel, 'Development Corporations in Aboriginal Communities: The Canadian Experience' (2009) 14(1) *Journal of Developmental Entrepreneurship* 1, 4.

DOI: 10.4324/9781003509066-6

Broadly, Indigenous claims to title over land are at bottom about sovereignty, not only land rights.[6]

The contemporary postcolonial experience of minority Indigenous Peoples in majoritarian settler countries is most relevant currently. This is not to gainsay the historic oppression of, say, Irish people or the continued economic colonialism in South Africa, but interest here lies with the Indigenous Peoples most obviously contemplated by the *United Nations Declaration on the Rights of Indigenous Peoples* (UNDRIP). Approximately 3.5% of the Australian population identifies as Indigenous, 5% of Canadians and 16.5% of people in New Zealand.[7] Settler members of postcolonial political communities must exercise their moral imaginations to try to understand to the extent possible how colonialism disrupted the social, economic and cultural systems of Indigenous Peoples, including the trade practices that were central to their lives and had developed over centuries, or possibly millennia in the case of First Australians.

Table 6.1 identifies different models of colonial and postcolonial regulation.

These broad categories are illustrative, non-exhaustive and porous at the boundaries. For example, settler governments often used both assimilation and authoritarian paternalism in different areas of regulation.[8] For postcolonial countries with settler majorities, the principal regulatory considerations are engagement with their colonial legacies and compliance with their UNDRIP undertakings.

If assimilation and authoritarian paternalism have been the primary ways of historic regulation of Indigenous Peoples, it is difficult for settler majority governments to abruptly adopt different approaches and to take their electorates with them.[9] New ways of regulating need to be negotiated and become embedded, ideally at a constitutional level because constitutions are difficult to change.[10] Differential, restorative treatment of Indigenous Peoples is espe-

6 See Andrew Erueti, *The UN Declaration on the Rights of Indigenous Peoples: A New Interpretative Approach* (Oxford University Press, 2022) 215.

7 See 'IWGIA', *International Work Group for Indigenous Affairs* (Web Page) <www.iwgia.org>. According to Stats NZ, the Māori population is close to 20% of the New Zealand population. See 'Māori population estimates: Mean year ended 31 December 2023 (2018-base)', *Stats NZ* (Web Page, 16 May 2024) <https://www.stats.govt.nz/information-releases/maori-population-estimates-mean-year-ended-31-december-2023/>.

8 In Queensland eg, between 1904 and 1939, the Chief Protector of Aboriginals Office 'managed the affairs of Aborigines deemed to be State wards, under a policy of protection and segregation'. See 'Chief Protector of Aboriginals Office', *Queensland Government* (Web Page) <https://www.archivessearch.qld.gov.au/agencies/A135>. From the 1930s, Protection Boards were restyled as Welfare Councils and were underpinned by a policy of assimilation. See AP Elkin, 'Aborigines and the Ministers' Welfare Council' (1951) 23(4) *Australian Quarterly* 9.

9 On the failure of the Voice referendum in Australia, see eg, Kirstie Wellauer, Carly Williams and Bridget Brennan, 'Why the Voice failed', *ABC* (Web Page, 16 October 2023) <https://www.abc.net.au/news/2023-10-16/why-the-voice-failed/102978962>.

10 Even the deeply entrenched rights of the Canadian Constitution are not immutable. See 'Amending Formula', *Centre for Constitution Studies* (Report,2019) https://www.constitutionalstudies.ca/2019/07/amending-formula/?print=print.

Table 6.1 Models of colonial and postcolonial regulation

Model	*Description (example)*	*Regulatory consequences*
Independence	Full withdrawal of colonial power (eg, Malaysia and Singapore, 1950s)	Colonial era regulatory norms persist but with localisation
Assimilation	Attempt to Westernise Indigenous People (eg, New Zealand before 1970s)[a]	Few distinctions between regulation of settler and Indigenous institutions
Authoritarian paternalism	Indigenous People treated as second-class citizens (eg, Australia before 1960s)[b]	Assertion of inferiority; State imposed regulation over wide areas of life
Confederation	Negotiated agreements with State(s) (eg, Canada from 1980s)[c]	Recognition of difference; differential regulation reached through negotiation and agreement
Federation	Indigenous People recognised as independent nations within a federal structure (eg, 'Indian' territories in the United States)[d]	Broad freedom to regulate in non-federal areas akin to states in a federation

[a]In 1975, the Waitangi Tribunal was established as a tribunal to inquire and make recommendations about claims regarding breaches by the Crown of its obligations under the Treaty of Waitangi/Te Tiriti o Waitangi 1840. See Treaty of Waitangi Act 1975 (NZ) ss 4 and 5.

[b]The Commonwealth Electoral Act 1918 (Cth) was amended by the Commonwealth Electoral Act 1962 (Cth) to permit Indigenous People to register to vote in Federal elections. Indigenous Peoples were not counted as Australians before the national census of 1971.

[c]See Constitution Act 1982 (Canada) s 35(1) which recognises and affirms 'existing aboriginal and treaty rights of the aboriginal peoples of Canada'.

[d]See *McGirt v Oklahoma* 591 US ___ (2020) on the independence of the Muscogee Nation from the state of Oklahoma.

cially susceptible to perceptions of unequal and non-democratic preference by majoritarian settler electorates,[11] yet compliance with UNDRIP requires a commitment to decolonising laws and institutions.[12]

11 See generally, Philip Pettit, 'Minority Claims under Two Conceptions of Democracy' in Duncan Ivison, Paul Patton and Will Sanders (eds), *Political Theory and the Rights of Indigenous Peoples* (Cambridge University Press, 2000) 199, 201, and specifically, Nadine Anne Hura, 'The prospect of co-governance sparks deep, irrational fears', *The Spinoff* (20 February 2020) <https://thespinoff.co.nz/atea/20-02-2023/the-prospect-of-co-governance-sparks-deep-irrational-fears>.

12 See generally, Erueti (n 6).

While restorative treatment of Indigenous Peoples may be unpopular with some in majoritarian settler states,[13] Australia, Canada and New Zealand have ratified UNDRIP. Art 19 provides:

> States shall consult and cooperate in good faith with the indigenous peoples concerned through their own representative institutions in order to obtain their free, prior and informed consent before adopting and implementing legislative or administrative measures that may affect them.

Of the broad regulatory approaches tabulated above, only versions of confederation or federation are plausibly compatible with the principles underpinning UNDRIP.

This chapter focuses on:

- Legacy – the extent to which postcolonial States may be prepared to overcome past behaviour to honour their UNDRIP obligations and to share sovereignty with the Indigenous Peoples of settled territories.
- The structure of current business entities that are expected to meet the needs of Indigenous Peoples.
- The possibility of a move towards regulatory confederation that complies with UNDRIP undertakings.

6.2 Colonial experience and UNDRIP

UNDRIP can only make sense to settlers if they have some understanding of colonialism. But however sympathetic settler members of postcolonial countries may be, they cannot share in the experiences of colonised Indigenous Peoples. The metaphor of a woman trapped in the nightmare of an abusive relationship throws light on the Māori experience of New Zealand's treaty-based colonisation.[14] True decolonisation – a *restitutio in integrum* expungement of colonialism – is not possible but critical analysis of structures of governance and how they unfairly impact on Indigenous Peoples is not only possible but necessary if restitutive justice is to be pursued. At its root, 'decolonisation is underpinned by a commitment to making cohabitation work'.[15] UNDRIP provides an indication of how this goal might be achieved.

13 For a discussion of majoritarianism, see James Allan, 'Majoritarianism' (2017) 29(2) *Bond Law Review* 1.

14 See Mike Ross, 'The Throat of Parata' in Bianca Elkington et al., *Imagining Decolonisation* (Bridget Williams Books, 2020) 21, 26–27.

15 See Ocean Ripeka Mercier, 'What Is Decolonisation?' in Bianca Elkington et al., *Imagining Decolonisation* (Bridget Williams Books, 2020) 40, 41.

The following sections provide thumbnail sketches of colonialism in Australia, Canada and New Zealand, then highlight how the different governments have engaged with the key principles of UNDRIP.

6.2.1 Australia

The Indigenous Peoples of Australia are generally thought to have maintained the oldest continuous culture on earth.[16] Australia has a huge landmass and is comprised of states and territories, but no state or territory has a majority population of Indigenous Peoples or permits autonomous governance. Expressions of ostensible imperial good faith in proclamations and treaties made elsewhere did not apply in the Australian colonies where the pernicious doctrine or terra nullius (unoccupied land) was practised.[17] The landmark *Wik* and *Mabo* decisions discredited terra nullius,[18] and paved the way for the *Native Title Act 1993* (Cth) whose preamble provides:

> The people whose descendants are now known as Aboriginal peoples and Torres Strait Islanders were the inhabitants of Australia before European settlement.
>
> They have been progressively dispossessed of their lands. This dispossession occurred largely without compensation, and successive governments have failed to reach a lasting and equitable agreement with Aboriginal peoples and Torres Strait Islanders concerning the use of their lands.
>
> As a consequence, Aboriginal peoples and Torres Strait Islanders have become, as a group, the most disadvantaged in Australian society.

Historical settler treatment of original Australians was appalling. If the term 'genocide' is possibly anachronistic,[19] massacres were nevertheless employed as a means of controlling Indigenous resistance.[20] Long into the twentieth century Indigenous Peoples were treated with an authoritarian paternalism that included 'stealing' children to be assimilated but subjugated within mainstream society.[21] That legacy is difficult to forget or forgive.

16 See eg, Christine Morris, 'Indigenous Intellectual Property Rights: The Responsibilities of Maintaining the Oldest Continuous Culture in the World' (1997) 4(2) *Indigenous Law Bulletin* 9.

17 On the origins of terra nullius, see Randall Lesaffer, 'Argument from Roman Law in Current International Law: Occupation and Acquisitive Prescription' (2005) 16(1) *European Journal of International Law* 25.

18 See *Mabo v Queensland* No 2 [1992] HCA 23; *Wik Peoples v Queensland* [1996] HCA 40.

19 See generally, Douglas Irvin-Erickson, *Raphael Lemkin and the Concept of Genocide* (University of Pennsylvania Press, 2017).

20 See eg, Andrew Markus, 'Genocide in Australia' (2001) 25 *Aboriginal History* 57.

21 See eg, 'Australia's Stolen Generations: Sorry Is Not Enough' (2018-09) 3(9) *The Lancet* e407. On forced sterilisation amounting to 'eugenics', see Laura Rademaker, Jakelin Troy and Julia

Not only were internal trade patterns disrupted by colonialism, so were long-established commercial relations with external traders from modern-day Indonesia.[22] It was not in the interests of settlers for Indigenous Peoples to live off the fruit of their lands and waters – they wanted cheap Indigenous labour.

While the Australian colonial legacy may appear to present insurmountable barriers to redress, Western Australia's *Noongar (Koorah, Nitja, Boordahwan) (Past, Present, Future) Recognition Act 2016* (WA) indicates that state governments can reject that legacy. The South West Native Title Settlement is the most significant land title settlement agreement in Australian history. Critically, the settlement allows for the creation of self-governing corporations, which effectively act as 'a fourth level of government' exercising 'powers and functions, not only in regard to aspects arising from traditional law and customs, but also in socio-economic fields such as housing, welfare, land management, conservation and tourism'.[23] The Noongar model may provide a template for other parts of Australia and beyond.

6.2.2 Canada

In terms of the UK Crown's 1763 Royal Proclamation,[24] North American First Nations retained rights to their lands unless those rights were extinguished by voluntary cession. In addition, the Crown concluded numerous treaties with First Nations in Canada,[25] notably 'in Ontario and the Prairie Provinces. But no such treaties exist for the Atlantic Provinces, or parts of Quebec, British Columbia, the Yukon, the Northwest Territories, as well for pockets of land elsewhere'.[26] Despite the Royal Proclamation, the settler government in British Columbia implausibly claimed terra nullius.[27]

Constitution Act 1982 (Canada) s 35(1) provides: 'The existing aboriginal and treaty rights of the aboriginal [Indigenous] peoples of Canada are hereby

---

Hurst; 'Friday essay: "too many Aboriginal babies" – Australia's secret history of Aboriginal population control in the 1960s', *The Conversation* (Web Page, 12 April 2024) https://theconversation.com/friday-essay-too-many-aboriginal-babies-australias-secret-history-of-aboriginal-population-control-in-the-1960s-189249.

22 See CC Macknight, *The Voyage to Marege': Macassan Trepangers in Northern Australia* (Melbourne University Press, 1976) 100–26.

23 See Bertus de Villiers, 'Privatised Autonomy for the Noongar People of Australia: A New Model for Indigenous Self-Government' in Lait Klain-Gabbay (ed), *Indigenous, Aboriginal, Fugitive and Ethnic Groups around the Globe* (IntechOpen, 2019).

24 See 'Royal Proclamation 1763: Relationships, Rights and Treaties', *Government of Canada* (2013) <www.rcaanc-cirnac.gc.ca/eng/1379594359150/1607905375821>.

25 See eg, *Mi'kmaq Peace and Friendship Treaty*, signed 15 December 1725 (entered into force 4 June 1726).

26 See Brian Slattery, 'The Hidden Constitution: Aboriginal Rights in Canada' (1984) 32(2) *American Journal of Comparative Law* 361.

27 See John Borrows, 'The Durability of Terra Nullius: Tsilhqot'in Nation v British Columbia' (2015) 48(3) *UBC Law Review* <https://commons.allard.ubc.ca/ubclawreview/vol48/iss3/2/>.

recognized and affirmed'. 'Section 35 contains a full box of rights, and holds the promise that Indigenous nations will become partners in Confederation on the basis of a fair and just reconciliation between Indigenous peoples and the Crown'.[28]

Following *Yahey*,[29] a landmark decision of the British Columbia Supreme Court, which found that the Crown had breached its obligations under a treaty with the Blueberry River nation, the British Columbia government agreed to pay C$800 million in compensation and conceded wide-ranging decision-making powers over the Nation's traditional lands. Provided a First Nation can demonstrate in court that the government has breached its treaty promises, it seems that compensation may be obtained and some control over lands can be regained. Even without a specific treaty, a First Nation may invoke the constitutionally vague Royal Proclamation and *Constitution Act* s 35.

The Truth and Reconciliation Commission (TRC) (2007–15) was established to investigate the horrific experiences of Indigenous children in the so-called Indian Residential School system.[30] The TRC Report shone a damning light on Canadian colonial practices, and recommended incorporation of UNDRIP into domestic law and practices, including in the field of business. The simple message was this: 'The way we do business must change'.[31]

Both the British Columbia and federal Parliaments have enacted statutes aimed at importing UNDRIP principles into domestic law.[32]

6.2.3 New Zealand

Before 1840, the islands of Aotearoa New Zealand comprised an agglomeration of cognate, independent Indigenous Peoples, with hapū (sub-tribe) being the normal socio-political unit.[33] The Crown, however, prefers to deal with iwi (tribes).[34] After the 1840 signing of the Treaty of Waitangi/Te Tiriti o

28 See 'Honouring the Truth,Reconciling for the Future', *Truth and Reconciliation Commission of Canada* (Report, 2015) <https://irsi.ubc.ca/sites/default/files/inline-files/Executive_Summary_English_Web.pdf 'Indigenous Peoples' comprise First Nations, Inuit and Métis.

29 See *Yahey v British Columbia* 2021 BCSC 1287.

30 See 'Honouring the Truth, Reconciling for the Future Summary of the Final Report of the Truth and Reconciliation Commission of Canada' (Report, 2015) (TRC) <https://ehprnh2mwo3.exactdn.com/wp-content/uploads/2021/01/Executive_Summary_English_Web.pdf>.

31 See ibid 317.

32 See *Declaration on the Rights of Indigenous Peoples Act* [SBC 2019] c 44 and *United Nations Declaration on the Rights of Indigenous Peoples Act* [SC 2021] c 14.

33 See 'Traditional Social Structure' in A McLintock (ed), An *Encyclopaedia of New Zealand* (Web Page, 1966) <https://teara.govt.nz/en/1966/maori-social-structure>.

34 See Natalie Coates, 'Infusing Tikanga into Corporate Māori Governance Entities in the Current Legal Framework' in Robert Joseph and Richard Benton (eds), *Waking the Taniwha: Māori Governance in the 21st Century* (Thomson Reuters, 2021) 137, 148.

Waitangi, New Zealand became a unitary state, although the country briefly experimented with provinces.[35] Akin to the Royal Proclamation, te Tiriti/the Treaty is a foundational constitutional document with debatable legal status.[36] Unlike Canada, New Zealand has no specific Māori 'reserves',[37] but, despite a long-term policy of assimilation, including in relation to land tenure,[38] compensatory settlement for breaches of the Treaty have seen iwi regain some control over traditional lands and natural resources.[39]

6.3 Indigenous corporations

This section outlines legislative efforts in Australia, Canada and New Zealand to structure business corporations that meet the needs of Indigenous Peoples.

6.3.1 Australia

The *Corporations (Aboriginal and Torres Strait Islander) Act 2006* (Cth) (CATSI Act) provides for a special form of incorporation for Aboriginal and Torres Strait Islander organisations under the auspices of the Registrar of Aboriginal and Torres Strait Islander Corporations.[40] The CATSI Act outlines governance requirements for Indigenous corporations registered under the Act. While some requirements were developed specifically to accommodate Indigenous traditions and circumstances, others are general in nature and aim to promote good governance and ensure accountability and transparency. A CATSI corporation, which must have Indigenous control,[41] is classified as

35 See Malcolm McKinnon, 'Colonial and provincial government', *Te Ara – the Encyclopedia of New Zealand* (Web Page, 6 October 2024) <https://teara.govt.nz/en/1966/maori-social-structure>.

36 See eg, Noel Cox, 'The Treaty of Waitangi and the Relationship between the Crown and Maori in New Zealand' (2002) 28(1) *Brooklyn Journal of International Law* 123. While ill-equipped to comment on the te reo Māori version, I am persuaded that neither the Māori nor English text of te Tiriti/the Treaty supports the view that iwi ceded 'sovereignty' (itself a European concept) to the Crown. See generally, Ned Fletcher, *The English Text of the Treaty of Waitangi* (Bridget Williams Books, 2022).

37 Canadian 'reserves' are similar to the better-known US 'reservations' and were mostly founded by the *Indian Act 1876.*

38 For a discussion of Māori land tenure under the conditions of colonialism, see RP Boast, 'Māori Land and Land Tenure in New Zealand: 150 Years of the Māori Land Court' (2016) 22 *Yearbook: New Zealand Association of Comparative Law* 77.

39 See generally, Christopher Finlayson and James Christmas, *He Kupu Taurangi: Treaty Settlements and the Future of Aotearoa New Zealand* (Huia, 2021).

40 See 'About us', *Office of the Registrar of Indigenous Corporations* (Web Page) <https://www.oric.gov.au/about-us>. See also Marina Nehme and John Francis Juriansz, 'The Evolution of Indigenous Corporations: Where to Now?' (2012) 33 *Adelaide Law Review* 101.

41 For a discussion of CATSI directors and their duties, see Marina Nehme, 'Indigenous Corporations and Accountability – the Evolution of the Directors' Duties' (2021) 36(3) *Australian Journal of Corporate Law* 240.

small, medium or large based on whether it meets the thresholds for any two of three criteria relating to income, assets and number of employees. However, the way a corporation reports to the Registrar is based on its size and income. This means it could be classified as small in terms of assets and staffing but has more reporting obligations because of its income.[42]

Soon after the CATSI Act came into force, the Aboriginal and Torres Strait Islander Social Justice Commissioner expressed concerns 'about the effects of the new CATSI Act on the exercise and enjoyment of Indigenous people's human rights', in particular 'that the CATSI Act does not undermine community control or confine Indigenous self-governance'.[43]

A 2017 technical review of the CATSI Act made some 70 recommendations for changes to CATSI corporations.[44] Most recommendations were technical in nature, but the call for simplifying reporting categories and greater structural flexibility was significant.[45] Furthermore, from a perspective of regulatory considerateness (see Chapter 5), the recommendation that 'all CATSI corporations be encouraged and supported to ensure that all directors have the necessary skills to manage their responsibilities' was noteworthy.[46] It was also recommended that:

> the replaceable rules be removed from the CATSI Act, but be replaced by one or more plain English model rule books. These model rule books would be default constitutions for a CATSI corporation. Further, it is recommended that there be at least one model rule book for [registered native title bodies corporate] and one for other corporations.[47]

The technical review was supported by a consultation report.[48] People consulted generally appeared less concerned about specific legislative provisions than with autonomy and self-determination, manifest in greater structural flexibility and the regulator principally playing a capacity-building, rather than enforcement, role.[49]

42 See 'Governance', *National Indigenous Australians Agency* (Report) <https://www.niaa.gov.au/sites/default/files/publications/catsi-act-governance-factsheet.pdf>.

43 See Aboriginal and Torres Strait Islander Social Justice Commissioner, 'Native Title Report 2007' (2007) 114.

44 See DLA Piper, 'Technical Review of the Corporations (Aboriginal and Torres Strait Islander) Act 2006' (Report, 2017) 2–20 <https://www.oric.gov.au/sites/default/files/TechnicalReviewCATSIAct_DLAPiper.pdf> ('Technical Review').

45 See ibid 2–3.

46 See ibid 6.

47 See ibid 2. See also Marina Nehme, 'A Comparison of the Internal Governance Rules of Indigenous Corporations: Before and After the Introduction of the Corporations (Aboriginal and Torres Strait Islander) Act 2006' (2014) 29(1) *Australian Journal of Corporate Law* 71.

48 See Inside Policy for the Office of the Registrar of Indigenous Corporations, 'The Corporations (Aboriginal and Torres Strait Islander) Act Review Consultation Report' (6 October 2017).

49 See 'Technical Review' (n 44) 232.

Academic research concludes that the CATSI Act should 'ensure that Indigenous Australians have a business structure that is culturally appropriate and fits their economic needs' and, because legislators have adopted an overly interventionist approach, 'the CATSI Act does not support Indigenous entrepreneurship and economic empowerment and therefore a review and a rethink of this approach is needed'.[50]

It is reasonable to conclude that Australia has not yet cut ties with its authoritarian paternalistic legacy in relation to Indigenous Peoples and their enterprises.

6.3.2 Canada

In addition to federal registration of companies, Canadian provinces and territories may register corporations under their own statutes. The possibility of crafting sub-national legislation that meets the needs of disparate Indigenous entrepreneurs and communities, therefore, presents as a more likely proposition than federal legislation. The population of Nunavut, for example, is just 33,320 but is almost 85% Inuit.[51] The territory has its own companies Act,[52] and provides for registration of Inuit businesses, which have preferential treatment for government procurement.[53] If the full suite of territorial business laws is inadequate, it seems plausible that legislation providing for a specific Inuit corporation could be enacted without democratic friction.

> Many business entities in First Nations communities are legally incorporated organizations – often called development corporations – set up and owned by the Band [First Nation] government on the reserves to serve the needs and goals of the local Band members and provide financial support for the community.[54]

More than 200 Indigenous economic development corporations (EDCs) 'exist across a range of industries such as retail, forestry, fisheries, energy, mining, construction, and hospitality. They have the potential to be major drivers for economic growth in Indigenous communities'.[55] Many EDCs are hybrid

50 See Marina Nehme, 'Aboriginal and Torres Strait Islander Corporations: Time for a Rethink?' (2023) 48(2) *Alternative Law Journal* 127, 132.

51 See 'Nunavut, Canada's Third Territory North of 60', *Government of Canada* (Web Page, 2024) <https://publications.gc.ca/collections/Collection/R34-6-1-1997E.pdf>.

52 See *Business Corporations Act*, SNWT (Nu) 1996, c 19.

53 See 'Inuit business and federal procurement', *Government of Canada* (Web Page, 2022) <https://www.sac-isc.gc.ca/eng/1646147382130/1648487162865>.

54 See Curry et al (n 5) 8.

55 See Christina E Hoicka and Matthew Foss, 'How Indigenous economic development corporations can support a just, low-carbon energy transition', *The Conversation* (Web Page, 27 June 2023) <https://theconversation.com/how-indigenous-economic-development-corporations-can-support-a-just-low-carbon-energy-transition-206976>.

organisations partnering with non-Indigenous resource corporations.[56] While EDCs are increasingly important economic actors, particularly in the field of renewable energy, the problems they present include:

- Maintaining the integrity of Indigenous culture in corporate governance, particularly in joint ventures with non-Indigenous enterprises.[57]
- Leakage of wealth from the community.[58]
- Lack of understanding of how the benefits of renewable energy are distributed.[59]

A further problem may lie with a lack of relevant regulation.

> Regulatory gaps exist where provincial regulatory regimes that relate to a proposed land use do not apply to reserve lands, and existing federal laws that apply to reserve lands do not fully address that particular commercial or industrial development. [*First Nations Commercial and Industrial Development Act 2005*] FNCIDA gives the federal government the ability to create a regulatory regime that clarifies and simplifies the rules for controlling an on-reserve project that is complex in nature. Regulations developed using the act ensure that environmental, health and safety, and other impacts of commercial and industrial developments are effectively managed throughout the life of the project.[60]

While FNCIDA may have the air of paternalistic regulation from the centre, the option lies with the relevant First Nation whether to elicit such support, which should ideally be confederal in nature.

In addition to commercial and regulatory concerns, legal and constitutional uncertainties abound.

> Because First Nations cannot create their own entities, the entities that they do employ inevitably become subject to private law, and engage as private entities, which reinforces the way that First Nations emerge as private actors in the economy, as passive interest holders or beneficiaries, as

56 See generally, Aidan R Vining and John Richards, 'Indigenous Economic Development in Canada: Confronting Principal-Agent and Principal–Principal Problems to Reduce Resource Rent Dissipation' (2016) 49 *Resources Policy* 358.

57 See generally, Frankie Young, 'Indigenous Economic Development and Sustainability: Maintaining the Integrity of Indigenous Culture in Corporate Governance' (2021) 17(2) *McGill Journal of Sustainable Development Law* 149.

58 See generally, Vining and Richards (n 56).

59 See Katarina Savic and Christina E Hoicka, 'Indigenous Legal Forms and Governance Structures in Renewable Energy: Assessing the Role and Perspectives of First Nations Economic Development Corporations' (2023) 101 *Energy Research & Social Science* 10321, 1.

60 'First Nations Commercial and Industrial Development Act', *Government of Canada* (Web Page, 2023) <https://www.sac-isc.gc.ca/eng/1100100033561/1612128155378>.

shareholders, but also as self-determining nations (and presumably 'entities') with rights under section 35 of the Constitution Act, 1982.[61]

6.3.3 New Zealand

New Zealand does not have a business entity specifically designed for Māori business.[62] This absence does not necessarily imply indifference on the part of government, rather it demonstrates the difficulties of implementing legal pluralism, specifically fluid and context-specific Indigenous customs, and protocols within the relatively rigid framework of Western company law.

In the early 2000s, the New Zealand Law Commission investigated a specific business entity to meet the business needs of iwi and hapū. Following the publication of the report,[63] the Waka Umanga (Māori Corporations) Bill was introduced in the last days of a Labour government. The incoming National government entered into a confidence and supply agreement with the Māori Party, which supported a first reading of the Bill to ascertain opinions from iwi and hapū. A leading textbook advises that the waka umanga initiative was 'ultimately unsuccessful largely due to it emerging well after most iwi and hapū had already established and embedded organisational structures holding complex asset portfolios'.[64] This explanation is incomplete. At the Committee stage, which follows the first reading of the Bill, the National Party made it clear it did not support further progress and the Māori Party expressed strong reservations about the Bill and withdrew its support. Representatives of the latter commented:

> the proposed waka umanga legal entity derails the possibility of hapū and iwi developing models of governance consistent with and expressive of tikanga Māori and tino rangatiratanga [sovereignty], and having those models duly recognised. We suggested that a more productive solution to current inadequacies could be found in Crown recognition of Māori governance entities, as formulated by hapū and iwi ... More work is needed to resolve the inadequacies of current legal structures. For any such programme to be fruitful, it will need to proceed from a kaupapa-Māori basis, and also address wider concerns with Treaty settlements policy.[65]

61 See Bradley Bryan, 'Indigenous Peoples, Legal Bodies, and Personhood: Navigating the "Public Body" Exemption with Private Law Hybrid Entities' (2020) 6 *Canadian Journal of Comparative and Contemporary Law* 58, 76.

62 A specific Māori entity, the 'incorporation' may be formed under *Te Ture Whenua Māori Act 1993* (NZ). However, incorporations may only hold land and may not engage in general business transactions.

63 See 'Waka Umanga: A Proposed Law for Māori Governance Entities' (NZLC R92, 2006).

64 See Elizabeth Macpherson, 'Iwi Companies' in Susan Watson and Lynne Taylor (eds), *Corporate Law in New Zealand* (Thomson Reuters, 2018) 111, 117.

65 See 'Waka Umanga (Māori Corporations) Bill Commentary', *New Zealand Legislation* (Report, 2007) <https://legislation.govt.nz/bill/government/2007/0175/24.0/DLM1593800.html>. The

The basic concern is that any new entity should be developed by and for Māori, and the critical consideration is that tikanga should inform the governance of the entity.[66] 'Tikanga' may be roughly translated as 'customary norms' but is highly contextual in terms of space, time and circumstance. It would be a foolhardy enterprise, for example, for a regulator to seek to codify tikanga.

Iwi widely use companies, but difficulties are faced in:

- Identifying individual shareholders.
- Balancing the interests of individual shareholders and communal shareholdings.
- Transferring shares.
- Engaging with fractionalisation of interests.[67]

Post Settlement Governance Entities (PSGEs) hold Treaty settlement assets. But before assets can be transferred, the Crown must be satisfied that a PSGE satisfactorily answers 'a list of 20 questions … to receive settlement assets'.[68] Despite this egregious paternalism, PSGEs have developed different ways in which to deal with tikanga. Inter-iwi enterprises, for example, have used the limited partnership (a body corporate-partnership hybrid)[69] as a joint venture vehicle because it is thought that a partnership agreement can better accommodate tikanga than a company constitution.[70] 'Each of these structures reflects the unique characteristics and emphasis of the iwi, including population, geography, tribal configuration, tikanga and history'.[71]

'Māori generally tend to try and make space, to the extent they can, to bend the Pākehā [European] framework to best suit them and to reflect elements of tikanga'.[72]

> Overall there is space for tikanga to operate in a real and meaningful way in the governance and day-to-day decision-making of corporate entities. That is through formal incorporation into governance documents; the

reference here is probably to the requirement that land receded by the Crown to iwi should be held by a particular entity, the Māori incorporation.

66 See Julie Cassidy, '"Frankenstein Incorporated" v Social Citizen: Learning from Māori Tikanga in Framing New Zealand Corporate Governance Principles' in Richard Benton and Robert Joseph (eds), *Waking the Taniwha: Māori Governance in the 21st Century* (Thomson Reuters, 2021) 205.

67 See Damian Stone, 'Maori Economic Development and Asset Utilisation' (2006) 1 *New Zealand Law Journal* 30, 31–32.

68 See ibid 30.

69 See *Limited Partnerships Act 2008* (NZ) s 11.

70 See Coates (n 34) 137.

71 See ibid 147.

72 See ibid 148.

discretion of the directors and decision-makers themselves; tribal pressure; and implied but potentially mandatory relevance.[73]

In the absence of Māori-led development of a specific corporate vehicle, iwi have crafted their own business structures, as exemplified by Ngāi Tahurrr arrangements. Ngāi Tahu is a large iwi (roughly 70,000 members) whose traditional lands cover the bulk of the South Island (Te Pounamu). The tribal economic group has net assets of NZ$1.78 billion.[74] The peak body, the Ngāi Tahu Charitable Trust (NTC Trust), is the ultimate shareholder of numerous business ventures, which are registered both as companies and charities, and make up a composite reporting body, the Ngāi Tahu Charitable Group. While general trusts do not have legal personality under New Zealand law and have a maximum 80-year term,[75] an exclusively charitable trust may apply for incorporation.[76]

The group's commercial companies are owned by the intermediary Ngāi Tahu Holdings Corporation Ltd. Like the other group companies, the constitution of the holding company prohibits the company and its directors, in their exercise of control, from engaging in 'any business other than as a trustee for the NTC Trust'.[77]

The three principal regulatory Acts that apply here pay scant attention to Māori interests. The *Charitable Trusts Act 1957* (NZ) omits any mention of Māori. The *Companies Act 1993* (NZ) allows the token use of 'Tāpui (Limited)' as opposed to 'Limited' as the last word(s) of a company name whose shareholders enjoy limited liability.[78] The *Charities Act 2005* grants charitable status to marae (meeting houses) under certain circumstances.[79]

6.4 Towards regulatory confederation

Legal pluralism is manifest when 'two or more legal systems coexist in the same social field'.[80] It is consistent with UNDRIP to recognise and respect Indigenous normative practices as laws within postcolonial legal systems.[81] Indeed, cognisance of worldviews different from the dominant Western

73 See ibid 152.
74 See Ngāi Tahu 2023 Annual Report.
75 For a discussion of the use of trusts in this context, see Stone (n 67) 31.
76 See *Charitable Trusts Act 1957* (NZ) s 7.
77 See Constitution of Ngāi Tahu Holdings Corporation Ltd (2016) [2.3].
78 See *Companies Act 1993* (NZ) s 21.
79 See *Charities Act 2005* (NZ) s 5.
80 See Sally Engle Merry, 'Legal Pluralism' (1988) 22(5) *Law & Society Review* 869, 870. For a review of legal pluralism and the jurisdictions considered in this chapter, see Kayleen M Hazlehurst, *Legal Pluralism and the Colonial Legacy: Indigenous Experiences of Justice in Canada, Australia and New Zealand* (Avebury, 1995).
81 See UNDRIP art 34. See also ILO Convention 189 Indigenous and Tribal Peoples in Independent Countries, arts 8 and 9.

perspective is an affirmation of the human rights that have particular relevance for Indigenous Peoples.[82] Regulatory confederation is a corollary of legal pluralism and is needed to ensure fullest promotion of social, economic and cultural rights. Indigenous Peoples may need statutes to be enacted so business vehicles may be created that meet their specific cultural needs, and which are subject to regulation different from mainstream corporations.

State concession does not apply in situations where Indigenous Peoples have retained sovereignty and so, akin to the organic conception of the corporation, it may be argued that Indigenous Peoples may create collective business vehicles as they wish in accordance with traditional customs and current needs. Nevertheless, the practical advantages of recognition of Indigenous business forms within the mainstream legal system – legal certainty being the primary consideration – appear to outweigh the moral benefits of asserting sovereignty over the formation and regulation of Indigenous corporations. Conversely, the State should recognise this concession and ensure that law and regulation of Indigenous business vehicles is confederal in nature.

Some regulatory issues appear to fall squarely within the State's purview, such as determining whether a foreign corporation should be permitted to carry on business in the relevant territory, and others should fall under the control of Indigenous Peoples, such as determining customary norms in a particular business context. But some issues overlap and here structures should enable the regulator and Indigenous Peoples to act in tandem.

The registration of trade marks in New Zealand provides an example of a small step towards regulatory confederation in the area of overlap between settler business and Indigenous interests. The Commissioner of Trade Marks must consult an advisory committee if a sign may be offensive to Māori.[83] The Commissioner is not obliged to follow the committee's advice but it would be highly unusual if they did not. The Registrar of Companies may refuse to reserve a company name they consider to be offensive.[84] In an instructive example, a trade mark for 'Naki' (a contraction of the name of the sacred mountain Taranaki) was refused but was accepted as part of a company name. While the trade mark registration refusal is welcomed, regulatory confederation would require joint structures and decision-making, not merely the provision of advice. The company names registration system should also manifest regulatory confederation.

Is a proposal for regulatory confederation just settler domination under another name? Indigenous Peoples have good grounds to be suspicious of attempts to envelop some Indigenous practices and knowledge – more

82 For an analysis of legal pluralism as a human right, see Eva Brems, 'Legal Pluralism as a Human Right and/or as a Human Rights Violation' in Giselle Corradi, Eva Brems and Mark Goodale (eds), *Human Rights Encounter Legal Pluralism: Normative and Empirical Approaches* (Bloomsbury, 2017) 23.

83 See *Trade Marks Act 2002* (NZ) s 178.

84 See *Companies Act 1993* (NZ) s 20(2)(d).

properly treasures – within mainstream law and to co-opt culture and sovereignty claims.[85] These concerns are valid but colonialism cannot be wished away. Ideally, sufficient spaces should exist for Indigenous Peoples to assert their full autonomy within postcolonial societies, and, within shared areas of sovereignty, good faith efforts can be made to co-create genuine confederal regulatory models. It is understandable that some Indigenous People do not want to be co-opted and will press for full and discrete sovereignty but, in counterpoint to this position, stand the majoritarian forces that may deny the special position of the original people of the land.

Bearing in mind that genuine regulatory confederation must be built from the ground up by the State and Indigenous Peoples together, and not anticipated and prescribed by majoritarian settlers, I propose the following suggestions:

- UNDRIP principles should inform law and regulations in a quasi-constitutional way.
- Laws and regulations should be co-designed. Financial reporting, in particular, should meet the needs of Indigenous communities and external stakeholders, rather than complying with abstract international financial reporting standards (IFRS). Of course, major Indigenous-controlled companies that operate in the mainstream economy should be expected to comply with IFRS.
- The nature of State regulation should be encouraging and aimed at capacity building, rather than policing and punishment.
- A long-term vision should be maintained of Indigenous Peoples fully regulating their corporations, with State cooperation if desired, considering the shift in costs and capacity issues.[86]
- Best practice notes should be developed jointly.
- When breaches of regulations do occur, application of Indigenous custom (as interpreted by appropriate learned elders) should provide the first response.
- The State should ensure that the rules governing non-Indigenous actors do not unduly impact on the legitimate interests of Indigenous actors and vice versa.

85 See eg, Ani Mikaere, *Colonising Myths: Māori Realities – He Rukuruku Whakaaro* (Huia, 2011) and Bianca Elkington et al., *Imagining Decolonisation* (Bridget Williams Books, 2020).

86 A funding conundrum exists. Indigenous Peoples may need greater funding from the State in order to develop structures and institutions necessary for autonomous governance, but central funding rarely comes without conditions which may themselves constrain autonomy. Government funding may, therefore, create a paternalistic 'top-down welfarism' type of governance structure. See Savic and Hoicka (n 59) 3.

6.5 Concluding comments

Indigenous Peoples must choose whether to forgive the postcolonial State and settlers for the transgressions of colonisation, and to seek to contribute to arrangements today that permit mutually beneficial cohabitation. In a context of broken promises, distrust and majoritarian backsliding, it is understandable that some Indigenous thought leaders wish to have nothing to do with compromise or further synthesis of laws and regulation. It is, however, a contemporary reality that postcolonial societies exist in which the original people of the land have been dispossessed and are now vastly outnumbered by settlers, and yet, to varying degrees and subject to the vicissitudes of the democratic will, in recent decades governments in Australia, Canada and New Zealand have generally taken some steps to make good historical misdeeds. But, following the models presented at the beginning of this chapter, regarding corporate regulation, only Canada has so far engaged with its UNDRIP obligations in ways that might eventually lead to genuine regulatory confederation. The legacy of authoritarian paternalism and an imaginative failure to co-develop laws and regulations that fully meet the needs and practices of Indigenous Peoples remain as formidable barriers to an UNDRIP-informed regulatory confederation.

7 Corporate regulation and technology

7.1 Introduction

Respect for human dignity demands that an individual must never be the instrument of another.[1] Conversely, a machine – however sophisticated – is no more than a tool for achieving human ends. Speculative fiction may present future possibilities when machines become indistinguishable in their appearance, intelligence, sentience and empathy from human beings, but those possibilities do not require current consideration. Today, machines are remarkable processors of information and far outstrip human capacity in that regard but are nevertheless just tools for achieving human ends.

This chapter reasserts the humanism that fundamentally informs this study. This version of humanism recognises the sentience of other animals and the critical importance of sustaining the ecosphere. Unlike machines made by human beings, flora and fauna are not, in essence, human instruments, and therefore deserve fullest ethical, legal and regulatory consideration. A proper analysis of this proposition lies beyond the scope of this study but for the foreseeable future, machines should be treated as instruments for human benefit. If we allow machines to usurp our autonomy, the human rights megalogue becomes enfeebled.

From a perspective of corporate regulation, certain technological developments deserve particular consideration.[2] One such development is the so-called 'smart contract', which uses distributed ledger technology (DLT) to bind parties into the future without further human action,[3] and 'regardless of the will of the parties'.[4] 'A smart contract is simply computer code … It

1 See Immanuel Kant, *Groundwork of the Metaphysics of Morals*, tr MJ Gregor (Cambridge University Press, 2006) 186–87.

2 For a fuller discussion of the relevant issues, see Jonathan Barrett, 'A Concession Approach to Distributed Ledger Enterprises' (2019) 25(1) *New Zealand Business Law Quarterly* 30.

3 For background on DLT, see Arvind Narayanan et al., *Bitcoin and Cryptocurrency Technologies: A Comprehensive Introduction* (Princeton University Press, 2016).

4 See ibid.

DOI: 10.4324/9781003509066-7

is not synonymous with a legally binding contract'.[5] Indeed, an arrangement that automatically executes, regardless of the will of the parties, is neither executed as planned nor consonant with *consensus ad idem*, the fundamental principle of contract law.[6] If the arrangement is to be legally enforceable, it must meet the traditional requirements of contract law.[7]

The corporate version of the smart contract is the decentralised autonomous organisation (DAO) for which decision-making is preordained by code. Akin to the DAO is the algorithmic entity for which decisions are also made by code. Collectively, these automatically executing arrangements may be referred to as code-based enterprises (CBEs).

Artificial intelligence (AI) is another significant technological development which, like smart contracts, is currently a misnomer. AI is essentially a remarkable way of iteratively processing and collating data that may present to the user as a form of thinking that massively exceeds human capacity. Whatever the future may hold, currently, 'under the hood' of AI is immense processing and assembling of data but it is neither artificial nor synthetic intelligence. However, since revolutionary technologies face a time lag before their useful potential is realised,[8] we may not see the full benefits and problematic issues of AI and corporate governance and regulation until the 2030s.

Neither CBEs nor AI can or should, under the conditions of current technology,[9] challenge human autonomous exercise of judgment and should not present an excuse for a failure to exercise directorial responsibility for the company and members of the political community.

7.2 Regulating cyberutopia

Despite its debt to the military,[10] the emergence of the Internet saw influential commentators go beyond free market liberal scepticism about government

5 See Chamber of Digital Commerce, 'Smart Contracts: Is the Law Ready?' (Report, September 2018) 22 <https://lowellmilkeninstitute.law.ucla.edu/wp-content/uploads/2018/08/Smart-Contracts-Whitepaper.pdf>.

6 Contracts are typically associated with the exercise of human autonomy. See Peter Nygh, *Autonomy in International Contracts* (Oxford University Press, 1999) 2. Autonomous contracting parties should be able to agree to novate the original agreement. To that extent, smart contracts may deny human autonomy.

7 Arizona, among other jurisdictions, has enacted specific smart contract legislation. See Arizona Revised Statutes 44-7003 (2017). The Smart Contracts Alliance, an initiative of the Washington-based Chamber of Digital Commerce, argues that such laws are unnecessary and unhelpful. Existing contract law can determine whether a so-called smart contract is a legal contract as such. Ibid.

8 See Paul Krugman, 'A.I. May Change Everything, but Probably Not Too Quickly', *The New York Times* (online, 31 March 2023) <https://www.nytimes.com/2023/03/31/opinion/ai-chatgpt-jobs-economy.html>.

9 For a history of AI and predictions for the future, see Robert H Chen and Chelsea C Chen, *Artificial Intelligence: An Introduction for the Inquisitive* (CRC Press, 2022).

10 See Evgeny Morozov, 'Two Decades of the Web: A Utopia No Longer', *Prospect* (online, 22 June 2011) <https://www.prospectmagazine.co.uk/ideas/technology/49273/two-decades-of-the

efficiency to espouse an ultra-libertarian,[11] anti-government and anti-regulation proposition – a cyberutopia in which terrestrial rules would be irrelevant and 'code is law'.[12] Cyberutopians argued that, since the Internet was unsuited to territorially based law, and traditional forms of regulation were likely to fail, cyberspace should be recognised as a distinct space with sui generis regulation,[13] if any. They commonly predicted a virtual space beyond the reach of terrestrial governments in which autonomous online communities would constitute and govern themselves.[14] A vainglorious *Declaration of the Independence of Cyberspace* asserted:

> We have no elected government, nor are we likely to have one, so I address you with no greater authority than that with which liberty itself always speaks. I declare the global social space we are building to be naturally independent of the tyrannies you seek to impose on us. You have no moral right to rule us nor do you possess any methods of enforcement we have true reason to fear.[15]

By the mid-2000s, the Internet had become a 'bordered network where territorial law, government power, and international relations matter as much as technological invention'.[16] Indeed, governments have shown both a willing-

---

-web-a-utopia-no-longer>. Furthermore, despite the anti-government rhetoric associated with crypto, governments are likely to be major users of the technology in the future. See 'How the blockchain can transform government', *Knowledge@Wharton* (Web Page, 5 July 2018) https://knowledge.wharton.upenn.edu/article/blockchain-can-transform-government/ .`

11 Ayn Rand appears to have been the most influential 'philosopher' in Silicon Valley. See eg, Nick Bilton, 'Silicon Valley's Most Disturbing Obsession', *Vanity Fair* (online, November 2016) <https://www.vanityfair.com/news/2016/10/silicon-valley-ayn-rand-obsession>; Lisa Duggan, *Mean Girl: Ayn Rand and the Culture of Greed* (University of California Press, 2019).

12 Lawrence Lessig coined the aphorism 'code is law' as a metaphor for the ways in which the programmed architecture of the Internet can have similar constraining effects on behaviour as law. See Lawrence Lessig, *Code Version 2.0* (Basic Books, 2006) ch 4.

13 See David R Johnson and David G Post, 'Law and Borders – The Rise of Law in Cyberspace' (1996) 48(3) *Stanford Law Review* 1367. The authors reiterated but clarified their arguments in David R Johnson and David G Post, 'The Great Debate – Law in the Virtual World' (2006) 11(2) *First Monday* <https://doi.org/10.5210/fm.v11i2.1311>.

14 See generally, Fred Turner, *From Counterculture to Cyberculture: Stewart Brand, the Whole Earth Network, and the Rise of Digital Utopianism* (University of Chicago Press, 2006). Of course, as in any movement, a spectrum of opinions and objectives exists. At the risk of presenting a straw-person argument, this chapter presents an arguably extreme version of cyberutopianism.

15 See John Perry Barlow, 'A declaration of the independence of cyberspace', *Electronic Frontier Foundation* (Web Page, 1996) <https://www.eff.org/cyberspace-independence>. Barlow admits his lack of democratic mandate in making his declaration.

16 See Jack Goldsmith and Tim Wu, *Who Controls the Internet?: Illusions of a Borderless World* (Oxford University Press, 2006) vii. See also Melissa de Zwart, 'The Internet in 2006: A Global, Corporate or Community Construct' (2006) 30(3) *Melbourne University Law Review* 1002. See

ness and capacity to restrict their citizens' online activities,[17] and to engage in surveillance of online activity on a grand scale.[18] Furthermore, the commercial aspects of cyberspace have become dominated by a small number of greatly unaccountable mega-corporations, notably Mega (Facebook), Amazon, Microsoft, Apple and Alphabet (Google). Despite this reality of monopolistic 'platform capitalism',[19] another upsurge in libertarian, anti-regulatory sentiment has occurred with the popularisation of crypto technology.

The failure of a prominent CBE indicates that significant financial markets issues may arise should CBEs proliferate. More generally, the neo-concession approach implies governments should intervene to set the conditions under which CBEs can operate in their jurisdictions. The trade-off for regulation might be conferral of legal personality on appropriately structured CBEs that agree to a socially beneficial level of transparency and disclosure, legal compliance and human oversight. This proposal echoes the Victorian response to ostensibly unregulable businesses (see Section 7.4).

7.2.1 The DAO – a failed CBE

A DAO is an organisation run through encoded rules. Governance is predetermined by 'smart contracts'. '*The* DAO' was a particular CBE built on the Ethereum decentralised blockchain,[20] which enables the use of smart contracts.[21] The DAO was designed to have no managers, legal documents or central server. Investors were required to trust code running on a distributed network of computers to invest the proceeds in projects approved by

---

also Uta Kohl, *Jurisdiction and the Internet: Regulatory Competence over Online Activity* (Cambridge University Press, 2007) 253; Petra Butler, 'When Is an Act of Parliament an Appropriate Form of Regulation? Regulating the Internet as an Example' in Susy Frankel and Deborah Ryder (eds), *Recalibrating Behaviour: Smarter Regulation in a Global World* (LexisNexis, 2013) 489.

17 See eg, Elizabeth C Economy, 'The Great Firewall of China: Xi Jinping's Internet Shutdown', *The Guardian* (online, 29 June 2018) <https://www.theguardian.com/news/2018/jun/29/the-great-firewall-of-china-xi-jinpings-internet-shutdown>.

18 See eg, Ally McCrow-Young, 'Visibility, Power and Citizen Intervention: The Five Eyes and New Zealand's Southern Cross Cable' (2017) 12(3) *Westminster Papers in Communication and Culture* 37.

19 See Nick Srnicek, 'The Challenges of Platform Capitalism: Understanding the Logic of a New Business Model' (2017) 23(4) *Juncture* 254.

20 Nathaniel Popper, 'Paper Points Up Flaws in Venture Fund Based on Virtual Money', *The New York Times* (online, 27 May 2016) <https://www.nytimes.com/2016/05/28/business/dealbook/paper-points-up-flaws-in-venture-fund-based-on-virtual-money.html>. See also Samuel Falkon, 'The Story of the DAO – Its History and Consequences', *Medium* <www.medium.com>; Kenneth Ng, 'Finding DAOism', *Medium* (Web Page, 29 June 2016) <https://medium.com/blockchainedu/finding-daoism-683246830c90>.

21 See Nathaniel Popper, 'A Venture Fund with Plenty of Virtual Capital, but No Capitalist', *The New York Times* (online, 22 May 2016) <https://www.nytimes.com/2016/05/22/business/dealbook/crypto-ether-bitcoin-currency.html>.

members. The tokens they received for their ether (the Ethereum cryptocurrency) gave the right to vote on proposals and receive rewards.[22]

Manifesting the cyberutopian ideal, The DAO was 'agnostic to borders, states, regulations, or government supervision',[23] and failed spectacularly. A flaw in the code, identified before its launch, allowed hackers to syphon off a third of investments.[24] The majority of investors opted to move to a new blockchain, while the fundamentalists stayed on the old system and so lost their investment but demonstrated loyalty to the principle that the blockchain is immutable.[25] After an investigation by the US Securities and Exchange Commission,[26] The DAO's promoters' belief that they had somehow created an investment vehicle for public subscription outside the remit of securities regulators was proved to be misplaced.

While much of the research and debate on CBEs has related to their internal control and governance,[27] State regulation of such arrangements is a crucial public concern.[28] We need to assert the rule of law over attempts to establish the rule of code or algorithm. Companies are not webs of contracts, and CBEs are not webs of smart contracts or chains of code. They are made possible by laws and must be appropriately regulated by the State and controlled by responsible human beings throughout their existence.

Regulatory problems do not only lie with minor rebellious groups such as those who devised The Dao, a critical issue for regulation lies with 'the commercialisation of cyberspace and the difficulties of any meaningful self-regulation in a space governed by technological giants'.[29] Governments of small countries may lack the technical expertise of mega-corporations, but private power must not be exempted from regulatory oversight.[30]

22 See Tanaya Macheel, 'The DAO might be groundbreaking, but is it legal?', *American Banker* (Web Page, 20 May 2016) <https://www.americanbanker.com/news/the-dao-might-be-groundbreaking-but-is-it-legal>.

23 See Bryan Smith, 'The story of the DAO, and how it shaped Ethereum', *Coin Insider* (Web Page, 23 May 2018) <www.coininsider.com>.

24 See ibid.

25 See Popper (n 21).

26 See WimlerHale, 'SEC confirms certain ICOs are securities offerings; regulators renew focus on cryptocurrencies', *Mondaq* (Web Page, 7 August 2017) <www.wilmerhale.com>.

27 See eg, Usman W Chohan, 'The Decentralized Autonomous Organization and Governance Issues', *SSRN* (Report, 2017, 2022) <https://papers.ssrn.com/sol3/papers.cfm?abstract_id=3082055>.

28 See eg, Nathan Tse, 'Decentralised Autonomous Organisations and the Corporate Form' (2020) 51(2) *Victoria University of Wellington Law Review* 313.

29 See Eliza Mik, 'Private Lawmaking in Commercial Cyberspace' (2016) 23 *Pandora's Box* 115, 119.

30 See ibid 125.

7.2.2 Algorithmic entities

Shawn Bayern has argued that an individual could confer legal personhood on an autonomous computer algorithm by putting it in control of a limited liability company (LLC).[31] 'The algorithm can exercise the rights of the entity, making them effectively rights of the algorithm'.[32] This argument appears to ignore the separate legal existence of a body corporate; nevertheless, it is imaginable that a regulatory competitive state might in the future, despite moral hazards,[33] register CBEs that are controlled purely by algorithms, rather than human directors.

7.3 Artificial intelligence

Current AI systems are not yet general-purpose thinking machines. They support specific tasks by analysing huge amounts of data 'to uncover patterns, reveal relationships, and make predictions for the purpose of augmenting human intelligence when provided with precise, quantifiable objectives set by systems engineers'.[34] Nevertheless, whereas tools and technology, from stone adzes to space rockets, have always enhanced our physical abilities, AI 'overcomes inefficiencies and limitations that stifle our biological *cognitive* abilities'.[35]

When the terms of the *Universal Declaration of Human Rights* were negotiated and related institutions created, an attempt was made to capture the broadest possible range of human ethical values.[36] In contrast, AI rules are set by systems engineers. Consequently, when 'AI models attempt to predict

31 See Shawn Bayern, 'The Implications of Modern Business Entity Law for the Regulation of Autonomous Systems' (2015) 19 *Stanford Technical Law Review* 93; Shawn Bayern et al., 'Company Law and Autonomous Systems: A Blueprint for Lawyers, Entrepreneurs, and Regulators' (2017) 9(2) *Hastings Science and Technology Law Journal* 135. See also Kelli A Alces, 'Beyond the Board of Directors' (2011) 46(4) *Wake Forest Law Review* 783; Matthew U Scherer, 'Of Wild Beasts and Digital Analogs: The Legal Status of Autonomous Systems' (2018) 19(1) *Nevada Law Journal* 259.

32 See Lynn M LoPucki, 'Algorithmic Entities' (2018) 95 *Washington University Law Review* 887, 890.

33 See European Economic and Social Committee, 'Artificial intelligence – The consequences of artificial intelligence on the (digital) single market, production, consumption, employment and society (own-initiative opinion), INT/806' (Report, 2019) <http://allai.nl/wp-content/uploads/2019/09/EESC-opinion-on-Artificial-Intelligence-and-Society.pdf>.

34 See Hong Qu, 'The Ends of Artificial Intelligence' in Seth Rudy and Rachel Scarborough King (eds), *The Ends of Knowledge* (Bloomsbury Academic, 2023) 139, 139. See also, David Runciman, *The Handover: How We Gave Control of Our Lives to Corporations, States and AIs* (Profile Books, 2023); Andrew Marantz, 'O.K., Doomer', *The New Yorker* (New York, 18 March 2024) 42.

35 See Qu (n 34) 148 (emphasis added).

36 See Julian Huxley, *UNESCO: Its Purpose and Its Philosophy* (UNESCO, 1946).

social outcomes … their surveillance, biases, and lack of transparency and accountability infringe on our human rights and impede equity'.[37]

At the time of writing, large language models are the best-known AI tools, and the key skill that people are expected to develop is 'prompt engineering'. Directors, for example, might prompt information on optimal financial reporting but they would still need to determine the usefulness and the accuracy of information produced. In company law, 'the good heart, empty head' doctrine in relation to incompetent but honest directors was once accepted.[38] Today, directors must be honest and competent. AI may be a useful tool to enable directors to work more efficiently, provided they can prompt knowledgeably and duly assess the information generated. We know, for example, that AI can generate spurious and biased information. Justified and proportionate differential treatment is permissible but 'inherently discriminatory processes will prevail in decision-making because of the evolutionary nature of some algorithms'.[39] To reiterate, AI exacerbates human bias. Are directors able to determine these deviances? How AI might help directors be more honest is not obvious given that the underpinning protocols are determined by coders, rather than ethicists, lawyers or experienced corporate controllers.

Worse than relying on faulty information, decision-makers might surrender their autonomy to automated, algorithm-based systems. Australia's Robodebt scandal, for example, arose from a public service initiative to automatically claw back money from benefit recipients who were identified by algorithms as likely fraudsters. The lesson that such systems must be transparent and subject to human oversight is relevant to commercial companies that may use algorithms for automated decision-making.[40]

The UN AI Advisory Board has issued high-level guiding principles. These include 'AI should be governed inclusively, by and for the benefit of all' and 'AI governance should be anchored in the UN Charter, International Human Rights Law, and other agreed international commitments such as the Sustainable Development Goals'.[41] On regulation, the Advisory Board observes, '[m]apping, avoiding, and mitigating risks will require self-regulation, national regulation, as well as international governance efforts. There should be no accountability deficits'.[42] It also notes that the ethical minimalism that characterises platform capitalist multinational enterprises is insufficient in the face of the potential risks posed by AI:

37 See Qu (n 34) 139.

38 See eg, *Re Cardiff Savings Bank* [1892] 2 Ch 100 (Marquess of Bute's case).

39 See Fotios Fitsilis, *Imposing Regulation on Advanced Algorithms* (Springer, 2019) 14.

40 See 'Royal Commission into the Robodebt Scheme Report Volume 1' (Commonwealth of Australia, 2023) xvi.

41 See UN AI Advisory Board, 'Interim Report: Governing AI for Humanity' (Report, 2023) <https://www.un.org/sites/un2.un.org/files/ai_advisory_body_interim_report.pdf>.

42 See ibid [35].

> 'Do no harm' is necessary, but not sufficient. A broader framing is needed for accountability of companies and other organisations that build, deploy and control AI as well as those that use AI across multiple sectors of the economy and society across the lifecycle of AI. This cannot rely on self-regulation alone: binding norms enforced by member states consistently are needed to ensure that public interests, rather than private interests, prevail.[43]

The International Science Council has developed a practical guide on engaging with AI for policymakers, but the series of questions it poses could also be adopted by directors to reflect on the position of the companies they control. Examples include:

- Autonomy: Could AI systems affect human autonomy by generating over-reliance by end-users?
- Human development: Is there an impact on acquisition of key skills for human development, such as executive functions or interpersonal skills, or changes in attention time affecting learning, personality development, mental health concerns?
- Societal values: Does the system fundamentally change the nature of society, enable normalisation of ideas previously considered anti-social, or breach societal values of the culture in which it is being applied?
- Social interaction: Is there an effect on meaningful human contact, including emotional relationships?
- Distorted realities: Are the methods used to discern what is true still applicable? Is the perception of reality compromised?
- Systems level of autonomy: How autonomous are the system's actions and what role do humans play?
- Degree of human involvement: Is there some human involvement to oversee the overall activity of the AI system and the ability to decide when and how to use the AI system in any situation?
- Evaluation: Are standards or methods available for evaluating system output?[44]

The *EU Artificial Intelligence Act 2023* aims to ensure that AI is 'safe, transparent, traceable, non-discriminatory, and environmentally friendly' and 'overseen by people, rather than by automation, to prevent harmful outcomes'.[45] The EU Act provides a full regulatory framework based on three categories: prohibited AI uses; regulated high-risk AI uses; and non-regulated,

43 See ibid [54].

44 See International Science Council, *A Guide for Policy-makers: Evaluating Rapidly Developing Technologies Including AI, Large Language Models and Beyond* (Paris, 2024).

45 See 'EU AI Act: first regulation on artificial intelligence', *European Parliament* (Web Page, 2023) <https://www.europarl.europa.eu/topics/en/article/20230601STO93804/eu-ai-act-first-regulation-on-artificial-intelligence>.

non-high-risk uses.[46] As supranational regulators, EU institutions benefit small Union members but, since the EU expects its AI Act to establish a global benchmark, non-EU countries could also adopt and adapt appropriate EU rules and models. For example, the EU has developed a tool to help small and medium enterprises (SMEs) assess their AI risks. A non-EU regulator could point SMEs in their jurisdiction to that tool.

7.4 Regulating the unregulable

The metaphor 'code is law' has become hackneyed and distorted; a cliché that implies computer code can supplant laws created by a democratically elected Parliament and courts subject to the rule of law:[47] for example, the code writer may be portrayed as a lawmaker because a smart contract they have programmed has automatic effects. But the code writer is no more a lawmaker than a drafter of a traditional contract is, and the code they write is not a law, any more than the text of a contract is law.[48] Code is simply a medium in which human instructions are recorded, within the framework of and in accordance with the rules of positive law. The careless code writer is legally answerable to their principal and affected others in the same way as a negligent draftsperson may be liable in contract or tort. A person who promotes interests in a code-defective CBE must be similarly responsible as a promoter of any other flawed business venture.

From a regulatory perspective, it is also important to recognise that code is not values-free:

> the architectural implementation of online platforms ultimately depends on the specific choices of platform operators and software engineers, seeking to promote or prevent certain types of actions. Just like any other technological artifact, code is not neutral but inherently political: it has important societal implications, insofar as it might support certain political structures or facilitate certain actions and behaviors over others.[49]

The common law can accommodate technological change,[50] and while CBE promoters may claim they have created something extra-legal, there is no

46 Cf 'Executive Order on the Safe, Secure, and Trustworthy Development and Use of Artificial Intelligence' (President of the United States, 30 October 2023).

47 See Christopher Millard, 'Blockchain and Law: Incompatible Codes?' (2018) 34 *Computer Law and Security Review* 843.

48 Cf copyright legislation, which includes a computer program as a 'literary work'. See eg, *Copyright Act 1994* (NZ) s 2(1).

49 See Samer Hassan and Primavera De Filippi, 'The Expansion of Algorithmic Governance: From Code Is Law to Law Is Code' (2017) 17 *Field Actions Science Reports* 88, 89, citing Langdon Winner, 'Do Artifacts Have Politics?' (1980) 109(1) *Daedalus* 121.

50 For a discussion of the common law's capacity to accommodate technological change, see Lyria Bennett Moses, 'Adapting the Law to Technological Change: A Comparison of Common Law and Legislation' (2003) 26(3) *University of New South Wales Law Journal* 394.

reason to think they have succeeded. If participants in a CBE share profits, as was planned for The DAO, they may be found to be partners with joint liability or joint venturers.[51] While joint venturers will normally face lower risks in relation to outsiders (depending, of course, on the functions they perform in the CBE), they may owe duties to their co-venturers.[52] In the light of these risks, incorporation may become attractive for CBE promoters,[53] but the State would need to have good reasons to concede such a right.

Ill-informed and heavy-handed regulation can stifle enterprise and socially beneficial developments along with detrimental possibilities. Some CBEs have, therefore, shown willingness to cooperate with State regulators, presumably to ward off further administrative or legal action.[54] These developments echo the concession to generally incorporate granted by the UK government in the mid-Victorian era.

Why did the State provide concessions to corporators in general?

One explanation is the particular form of the corporation was economically determined, and government simply recognised an irresistible force.[55] Another explanation is concession in the nineteenth century was linked to a social and political need for regulation. The Victorian laissez-faire business world may have been 'unregulable',[56] and fraud against passive investors was rife.[57] In enacting the *Joint Stock Companies Act*, government 'sought to protect the rentier investor'.[58]

> The Act … was aimed not at encouraging JSC [joint stock company] formation but at trying to protect rentier shareholders from fraud. To this end, it sought to compel JSCs to incorporate and to provide detailed information about their operations. The hope was that compulsory incorporation coupled with 'publicity' (what we would now call 'disclosure') would provide rentiers with the information they needed to make better informed investment decisions.[59]

51 See Dirk A Zetzsche, Ross P Buckley and Douglas W Arner, 'The Distributed Liability of Distributed Ledgers: Legal Risks of Blockchain' [2017] *University of New South Wales Research Study* 1, 32.

52 See eg, *Chirnside v Fay* [2007] NZSC 68.

53 See Philipp Hacker, 'Corporate Governance for Complex Cryptocurrencies? A Framework for Stability and Decision Making in Blockchain-Based Organizations' *SSRN* (2017) <www.papers.ssrn.com>. In practice, like many companies, CBEs might adopt off-the-rack constitutions.

54 See Fitsilis (n 39) 54.

55 See Reinier Kraakman et al., *Anatomy of Corporate Law* (Oxford University Press, 2004) 1.

56 See John Braithwaite, 'The Regulatory State?' in Robert E Goodin (ed), *The Oxford Handbook of Political Science* (Oxford University Press, 2011) 217, 218.

57 See eg, James Taylor, 'Criminalising Fraud: Victorian Responses to Company Scandals' (2011) 32(10) *Company Lawyer* 291.

58 See Paddy Ireland, 'Limited Liability, Shareholder Rights and the Problem of Corporate Irresponsibility' (2010) 34 *Cambridge Journal of Economics* 837, 843.

59 Braithwaite (n 56) 218.

Whether the mid-century corporate concessions had the effects government intended, they appear to have been made to bring ostensibly unregulable businesses within the regulatory net. The historical concessions might also indicate ways of engagement with crypto and other CBEs.

Legal personality could be granted to CBEs provided they are sufficiently similar in substance to corporations, and they earn the privilege.[60] The common characteristics of modern corporations are legal personality, limited liability, transferable shares, delegated management under a board structure and investor ownership.[61] Minus the concessions of legal personality and limited investor liability, The DAO manifested characteristics that can be plausibly likened to a modern corporation – pooled investment, transferability of interests and separation of ownership and control.

Limited investor liability for enterprise debts is a further privilege conferred by the State, notably to shareholders[62] and limited partners.[63] While it has long been questioned on the grounds of moral hazard whether shareholders in private companies should enjoy limited liability,[64] limited liability is widely thought to be economically efficient.[65] Certainly, the costs and benefits of granting limited liability to CBE investors should be properly considered but, in principle, 'there appears to be no compelling reason against an expansion of the menu of governance options available to firms doing business under the shield of limited liability'.[66] The critical point is that CBEs earn these concessions, for example, by committing to disclosure to a regulator, tax compliance, respecting human rights and protecting the interests of employees and creditors.[67] Most of all, responsible humans must control every phase of the organisation's existence.

7.5 Concluding comments

This chapter has sought to link historical experience with contemporary CBEs. Despite a largely unregulable, laissez-faire business context, *Salomon's case* confirmed the limited liability company as a creature of statute, immune,

60 See Max Ganado, 'Legal personality for blockchains, DAOs and smart contracts', *Mondaq Business Briefing* (Web Page, 6 June 2018) <https://www.mondaq.com/fin-tech/707696/legal-personality-for-blockchains-daos-and-smart-contracts>.

61 See Kraakman et al (n 55) 1.

62 See eg, *Companies Act 1993* (NZ) s 97.

63 See *Limited Partnerships Act 2008* (NZ) s 31.

64 See generally, Otto Kahn-Freund, 'Reflections on Company Law Reform' (1944) 7(1/2) *Modern Law Review* 54.

65 See eg, Frank H Easterbrook and Daniel R Fischel, 'Limited Liability and the Corporation' (1985) 52(1) *University of Chicago Law Review* 89.

66 See William W Bratton and Joseph A McCahery, 'An Inquiry into the Efficiency of the Limited Liability Company: Of Theory of the Firm and Regulatory Competition' (1997) 54 *Washington and Lee Law Review* 629, 635.

67 See Ganado (n 60).

under normal circumstances, from common law or equitable challenge.[68] The decision brought a high degree of certainty, and recognised Parliament's concession of legal personality to small enterprises in exchange for entrepreneurs accepting the form of the company prescribed by statute and submitting to regulatory oversight.

CBE promoters may claim they lie beyond regulation; their code is law; and securities legislation does not apply to them. Such regulatory secessionism cannot be countenanced in any democracy governed by the rule of law. But the freedom, autonomy and creativity of CBE entrepreneurs should also be respected and nurtured. A regulatory framework for CBEs should enable, rather than stifle, innovation and provide appropriate protection for all stakeholders. Conceding legal personality to CBEs which are substantially similar to companies, including autonomous human control, may be an appropriate trade-off for bringing these organisations within the regulatory net, with the requirements for disclosure and compliance such inclusion implies.

68 See Lord Sumption's explanation of lifting and piercing the corporate veil in *Prest v Petrodel Resources Ltd* [2013] UKSC 34.

8 Conclusion

This study has sought to weave together various strands of human experience and practices, both in general social life and business, to present a model of corporate regulation suitable for the contemporary context. The golden thread is the humanism that informs the constitutive rights affirmations of the *International Bill of Human Rights* (IBHR). These affirmations, in turn, establish the fundamental rules for the human rights State, which has committed itself to the IBHR, its agencies and its citizens. Human rights are not lofty ethical ideals; they provide practical guidelines for government and our everyday interactions, including our roles as corporate actors.

The neo-concession proposition presented in this study reasserts the concessionist legal fact that incorporation is only possible because a competent jurisdiction permits it but contextualises that fact, principally within the human rights environment but also within the contemporary business world.

I have rejected the idea of the company as a 'good corporate citizen'; that image presents as a progressive version of anthropomorphism. All human corporate actors must comply with their responsibilities as citizens of the human rights State, but companies are not citizens. Corporations hold property on behalf of investing shareholders. This is a matter of legal convenience. Allowing corporations to have standing to protect 'vicarious' proprietary interests by claiming rights enshrined in bills of rights is also a matter of convenience. If, for example, a State agency has unjustifiably confiscated investors' property pooled in the company, it is useful and appropriate for the company to be able to sue, rather than numerous shareholders.

Unlike typical studies of the company, I have sought to marginalise corporate theory. While engaging with different theoretical perspectives on this most challenging area may be intellectually stimulating, little of practical value is gained from deriving concepts in an area of human activity which is most obviously characterised by the untheorised pragmatism of businesspeople. The legal concerns that are most likely to exercise the minds of company directors are not included in corporate statutes, rather they lie in super-statutes, such as those governing offers of securities to the public, taxation, consumer protections, health and safety, environmental protection and competition law, since breaches of these Acts can lead to large corporate fines and possible

DOI: 10.4324/9781003509066-8

imprisonment for directors. These concerns mostly relate to business functions, rather than corporate capacity.

Although I have sought to marginalise corporate theories, most have some value. Organic theory, for example, alerts us to the need to ensure that the model of the company as statutorily enshrined is not irretrievably at odds with the model that business commerce would construct themselves. Similarly, contract theory alerts us to the problems of agency and the need to ensure directors and managers do not act unjustifiably in their own interests. Enterprise theories are consilient with the law, and usefully present the possibility of a corporate purpose beyond shareholder wealth maximisation. Real entity and team production theories situate the for-profit corporation within the greater realm of business organisations and the challenges they present for individual autonomy and society in general. None of these models is incompatible with State regulation. The cyberutopian rejection of State oversight is not, however, congruent with a perception of regulation that not only protects citizens from unjustified State and private interference, but also actively seeks to protect and promote citizens' human rights.

Legislative and regulatory considerateness is an important concern of this study. The goal of human rights lies in the flourishing of everyone within their political communities, subject to respect for other community members' rights and expectations. Legislation and regulatory practices should therefore help corporate actors become virtuous or excellent in their roles. This consideration is particularly important for controllers of small and medium enterprise companies who may wish to be cooperative but are incompetent in complying with the law and regulations.

Concessionism relies on a presumption that the State possesses the sovereign power to permit incorporation of qualifying arrangements. In postcolonial countries, this presumption may be misplaced because Indigenous Peoples may not have ceded sovereign rights over their lands. Neo-concessionism embraces legal pluralism as a contextual feature of the human rights State. The *UN Declaration on the Rights of Indigenous Peoples* (UNDRIP) indicates ways in which majority settlers and Indigenous Peoples can develop laws and regulations that move towards confederal arrangements. The principles of UNDRIP demand that space must be found for Indigenous-crafted forms of corporations that are sufficiently flexible to accommodate traditional and developing customary values and practices.

Technological developments potentially threaten the exercise of autonomy and the assumption of responsibility. These behavioural characteristics lie at the root of humanism. While we should foster innovation both in technology and regulation, we should never lose sight of what makes us human. Code is not a replacement for law, smart contracts should be subservient to the law of contract, and, for the foreseeable future AI should be recognised as a useful tool, not a substitute for honest and prudent judgment. This imperative has pressing relevance for the control of corporations.

The principal aim of this study was to establish the crucial importance of human rights in our consideration and construction of corporate regulation and to highlight areas of especial concern. Canonical or exhaustive statements on any of the issues raised were not intended. Nevertheless, I hope that this work will encourage debate and further research in this important field.

Bibliography

Articles/Books/Reports

Alces, Kelli A, 'Beyond the Board of Directors' (2011) 46(4) *Wake Forest Law Review* 783

Allan, James, 'Majoritarianism' (2017) 29(2) *Bond Law Review* 1

'Amending Formula', *Centre for Constitution Studies* (Report) <https://www.constitutionalstudies.ca/2019/07/amending-formula/?print=print>

'An Inquiry into the Application of the United Nations Declaration on the Rights of Indigenous Peoples (UNDRIP) in Australia', *Parliament of Australia* (Report) <https://www.aph.gov.au>

Arendt, Hannah, *The Origins of Totalitarianism* (3rd ed, Harcourt, Brace, 1967)

Asch, Michael (ed), *Aboriginal and Treaty Rights in Canada: Essays on Law, Equality, and Respect for Difference* (University of British Columbia Press, 1997)

A Sustainable Finance Policy Engagement Handbook (UNPRI, 28 November 2022)

'Australia's Stolen Generations: Sorry is not Enough' (2018–09) 3(9) *The Lancet* e407–e407

Ayres, Ian and John Braithwaite, *Responsive Regulation: Transcending the Deregulation Debate* (Oxford University Press, 1992)

Baerentzen, Susi, *The Effectiveness of General Anti-Avoidance Rules Their Limits, Challenges and Potential in EU and International Tax Law* (IBFD, 2022)

Baldwin, Robert, Martin Cave and Martin Lodge (eds), *The Oxford Handbook of Regulation* (Oxford University Press, 2010)

Barak, Aharon, 'Proportional Effect: The Israeli Experience' (2007) 57(2) *University of Toronto Law Journal* 369

Barrett, Jonathan, 'A Concession Approach to Distributed Ledger Enterprises' (2019) 25(1) *New Zealand Business Law Quarterly* 30

Barrett, Jonathan, 'Copying Artistic Works: Copyright, Aesthetics, and Artistic Practice' in Jani McCutcheon and Fiona McGaughey (eds), *Research Handbook on Art and Law* (Edward Elgar, 2020) 59

Barrett, Jonathan, 'Metaphysics and the Corporation' (2020) 35(3) *Australian Journal of Corporate Law* 305

Barrett, Jonathan, 'The Regulatory Challenges of Pseudo-foreign Corporations and Pseudo-corporations: A Neo-concession Approach' (2022) 38(1) *Australian Journal of Corporate Law* 1

Barrett, Jonathan, 'Company Names: Challenges for the Regulator' (2023) 39(1) *Australian Journal of Corporate Law* 1

Bauman, Zygmunt, 'The Absence of Society' in David Utting (ed), *Contemporary Social Evils* (Policy Press for Joseph Rowntree Foundation, 2009) 149

Bayern, Shawn, 'The Implications of Modern Business Entity Law for the Regulation of Autonomous Systems' (2015) 19 *Stanford Technical Law Review* 93

Bayern, Shawn, et al., 'Company Law and Autonomous Systems: A Blueprint for Lawyers, Entrepreneurs, and Regulators' (2017) 9(2) *Hastings Science and Technology Law Journal* 135

Belle Isle, Melissa, Brett Freudenberg and Tapan Sarker, 'The Business Tax Literacy of Australian Small Businesses' (2022) 37(1) *Australian Tax Forum* 65

Berlin, Isaiah, 'Two Concepts of Liberty' in Michael J Sandel (ed), *Liberalism and Its Critics* (Blackwell, 1984) 15

Bingham, Tom, *The Rule of Law* (Penguin Books, 2011)

Blair, Margaret M and Lynn A Stout, 'A Team Production Theory of Corporate Law' (1999) 85(2) *Virginia Law Review* 247

Blind, Peri K, 'Building Trust in Government: Linking Theory with Practice' in G Shabbir Cheema and Vesselin Popovski (eds), *Building Trust in Government: Innovations in Governance Reform in Asia* (United Nations University Press, 2010) 2

Boast, RP, 'Māori Land and Land Tenure in New Zealand: 150 Years of the Māori Land Court' (2016) 22 *Yearbook: New Zealand Association of Comparative Law* 77

Bonham, David H and Daniel A Soberman, 'The Nature of Corporate Personality' in Jacob S Ziegel (ed), *Studies in Canadian Company Law* (Butterworths, 1967) 5

Borrows, John, 'The Durability of Terra Nullius: Tsilhqot'in Nation v British Columbia' (2015) 48(3) *UBC Law Review* <commons.allard.ubc.ca/ubclawreview/vol48/iss3/2/>

Botha, Henk, 'Freedom and Constraint in Constitutional Adjudication' (2004) 20(2) *South African Journal on Human Rights* 249

Bottomley, Stephen, 'Taking Corporations Seriously: Some Considerations for Corporate Regulation' (1990) 19(3) *Federal Law Review* 203

Bovens, Mark, 'The Corporate Republic: Complex Organizations and Citizenship' in Emilios A Christodoulides (ed), *Communitarianism and Citizenship* (Ashgate, 1998) 158

Braithwaite, John, *Regulatory Capitalism: How It Works, Ideas for Making It Work Better* (Edward Elgar, 2008)

Braithwaite, John, 'The Regulatory State?' in R Goodin (ed), *The Oxford Handbook of Political Science* (Oxford University Press, 2009) 407

Braithwaite, Valerie, 'Closing the Gap between Regulation and the Community' in Peter Drahos (ed), *Regulatory Theory: Foundations and Applications* (ANU Press, 2017) 25

Bratton Jr, William W, 'The "Nexus of Contracts" Corporation: A Critical Appraisal' (1989) 74(3) *Cornell Law Review* 407

Bratton Jr, William W, 'The New Economic Theory of the Firm: Critical Perspectives from History' (1989) 41(6) *Stanford Law Review* 1471

Bratton, William W and Joseph A McCahery, 'An Inquiry into the Efficiency of the Limited Liability Company: Of Theory of the Firm and Regulatory Competition' (1997) 54 *Washington and Lee Law Review* 629

Brems, Eva, 'Legal Pluralism as a Human Right and/or as a Human Rights Violation' in Giselle Corradi, Eva Brems and Mark Goodale (eds), *Human Rights Encounter Legal Pluralism: Normative and Empirical Approaches* (Bloomsbury, 2017) 23

Brennan, Gerard, 'The Third Branch and the Fourth Estate' (1997) 32 *Irish Jurist* 62

Brown, Lesley, 'Introduction' in Aristotle, *The Nicomachean Ethics*, tr David Ross (OUP Oxford, 2009) i

Brownlie, Ian, *Principles of Public International Law* (6th ed, Oxford University Press, 2003)

Bryan, Bradley, 'Indigenous Peoples, Legal Bodies, and Personhood: Navigating the "Public Body" Exemption with Private Law Hybrid Entities' (2020) 6 *Canadian Journal of Comparative and Contemporary Law* 58

Buhmann, Karin, 'Public Regulator and CSR: The "Social Licence to Operate" in Recent United Nations Instruments of Business and Human Rights and the Juridification of CSR' (2016) 136(4) *Journal of Business Ethics* 699

Burke, Edmund, *Reflections on the Revolution in France* (Yale University Press, 2003, first published 1790)

Butler, Andrew and Petra Butler, *The New Zealand Bill of Rights Act: A Commentary* (2nd ed, LexisNexis NZ, 2005)

Butler, Petra, 'Rights and Regulation' in Susy Frankel (ed), *Learning from the Past, Adapting for the Future: Regulatory Reform in New Zealand* (Lexis Nexis, 2011) 241

Cassidy, Julie, '"Frankenstein Incorporated" v Social Citizen: Learning from Māori Tikanga in Framing New Zealand Corporate Governance Principles' in Richard Benton and Robert Joseph (eds), *Waking the Taniwha: Māori Governance in the 21st Century* (Thomson Reuters, 2021) 205

Chamber of Digital Commerce, 'Smart Contracts: Is the Law Ready?' (Report, September 2018) <https://lowellmilkeninstitute.law.ucla.edu/wp-content/uploads/2018/08/Smart-Contracts-Whitepaper.pdf>

Chen, Robert H and Chelsea C Chen, *Artificial Intelligence: An Introduction for the Inquisitive* (CRC Press, 2022)

'Chief Protector of Aboriginals Office', *Queensland Government* (Report) <https://www.archivessearch.qld.gov.au/agencies/A135>

Chiu, Iris H-Y, 'An Institutional Theory of Corporate Regulation' (2018) 71(1) *Current Legal Problems* 279

Chohan, Usman W, 'The Decentralized Autonomous Organization and Governance Issues' *SSRN* (Report, 2017, 2022) <https://papers.ssrn.com/sol3/papers.cfm?abstract_id=3082055>

Cilliers, HS, et al., *Corporate Law* (2nd ed, Butterworths, 1992)

Clapham, Andrew, *Human Rights and Non-State Actors* (Edward Elgar, 2013)

Coates, Natalie, 'Infusing Tikanga into Corporate Māori Governance Entities in the Current Legal Framework' in Robert Joseph and Richard Benton (eds), *Waking the Taniwha: Māori Governance in the 21st Century* (Thomson Reuters, 2021) 137

Cohen, David L, 'Theories of the Corporation and the Limited Liability Company: How Should Courts and Legislatures Articulate Rules for Piercing the Veil, Fiduciary Responsibility and Securities Regulation for the Limited Liability Company' (1998) 51 *Oklahoma Law Review* 427

Cohen, Joanna E, et al., 'Plain Packaging of Tobacco Products: Lessons for the Next Round of Implementing Countries' (2020) 18 *Tobacco Induced Diseases* 94

Cohen, Richard A, 'Introduction' in Emmanuel Levinas, *Humanism of the Other*, tr N Poller (University of Illinois Press, 2003) i

Constitution of Ngāi Tahu Holdings Corporation Ltd (2016)

Cord, Robert A, *The Palgrave Companion to Chicago Economics* (Springer, 2023)
Cornell, Stephen, et al., 'Citizen Entrepreneurship: An Underutilized Development Resource' in Miriam Jorgensen (ed), *Rebuilding Native Nations: Strategies for Governance and Development* (University of Arizona Press, 2007) 197
Cotterrell, Roger, *The Politics of Jurisprudence: A Critical Introduction to Legal Philosophy* (University of Pennsylvania Press, 1989)
Cox, Noel, 'The Treaty of Waitangi and the Relationship Between the Crown and Maori in New Zealand' (2002) 28(1) *Brooklyn Journal of International Law* 123
Cox, Susan Jane Buck, 'No Tragedy on the Commons' (1985) 7(1) *Environmental Ethics* 49
Currie, Iain and Jonathan Klaaren, *The Promotion of Administrative Justice Act Benchbook* (SiberInk, 2001)
Curry, John, Han Donker and Richard Krehbiel, 'Development Corporations in Aboriginal Communities: The Canadian Experience' (2009) 14(1) *Journal of Developmental Entrepreneurship* 1
Davies, Tony, *Humanism* (Routledge, 1997)
de Villiers, Bertus, 'Privatised Autonomy for the Noongar People of Australia: A New Model for Indigenous Self-Government' in Lait Klain-Gabbay (ed), *Indigenous, Aboriginal, Fugitive and Ethnic Groups Around the Globe* (IntechOpen, 2019)
de Zwart, Melissa, 'The Internet in 2006: A Global, Corporate or Community Construct' (2006) 30(3) *Melbourne University Law Review* 1002
Dias, RWM, *Jurisprudence* (4th ed, Butterworths, 1976)
Diephuis, JH, 'Recognition of Foreign Companies and Bodies Corporate: The Concept of Recognition, a Short Historical Review and a Critical Analysis of the Main Provisions of the EEC Recognition Convention' (2009) 27(3) *Netherlands International Law Review* 347
DLA Piper, 'Technical Review of the Corporations (Aboriginal and Torres Strait Islander) Act 2006' (Report, 2017) <https://www.oric.gov.au/sites/default/files/TechnicalReviewCATSIAct_DLAPiper.pdf>
Dodd Jr, E Merrick, 'For Whom Are Corporate Managers Trustees?' (1932) 45(7) *Harvard Law Review* 1145
Drahos, Peter (ed), *Regulatory Theory: Foundations and Applications* (ANU Press, 2017)
Duggan, Lisa, *Mean Girl: Ayn Rand and the Culture of Greed* (University of California Press, 2019)
Eagleton, Terry, *Literary Theory: An Introduction* (University of Minnesota Press, 1983)
Easterbrook, Frank H and Daniel R Fischel, 'Limited Liability and the Corporation' (1985) 52(1) *University of Chicago Law Review* 89
Edwards, P and S Trafford, 'Social Licence in New Zealand – What is it?' (2016) 46 (3–4) *Journal of the Royal Society of New Zealand* 165
Eisenhardt, Kathleen M, 'Agency Theory: An Assessment and Review' (1989) 14(1) *Academy of Management Review* 57
Elkin, AP, 'Aborigines and the Ministers' Welfare Council' (1951) 23(4) *Australian Quarterly* 9
Elkington, Bianca, et al., *Imagining Decolonisation* (Bridget Williams Books, 2020)
Emberland, Marius, *The Human Rights of Companies: Exploring the Structure of ECHR Protection* (Oxford University Press, 2006)

Erueti, Andrew, *The UN Declaration on the Rights of Indigenous Peoples: A New Interpretative Approach* (Oxford University Press, 2022)

Eskridge, Jr, William N and John Ferejohn, 'Super-Statutes' (2001) 50(5) *Duke Law Journal* 1215

Etzioni, Amitai, 'Introduction' in Amitai Etzioni and David E Carney (eds), *Repentance: A Comparative Perspective* (Rowman & Littlefield, 1997) 1

European Economic and Social Committee, 'Artificial Intelligence – The Consequences of Artificial Intelligence on the (digital) Single Market, Production, Consumption, Employment and Society (Own-initiative Opinion), INT/806' (Report, 2019) <http://allai.nl/wp-content/uploads/2019/09/EESC-opinion-on-Artificial-Intelligence-and-Society.pdf>

'Fact Sheet No.2 (Rev.1), 'The International Bill of Human Rights' *OHCHR* (Report, 1996) <https://www.ohchr.org/Documents/Publications/FactSheet2Rev.1en.pdf>

Fenton, William N, 'This Island, the World on the Turtle's Back' (1962) 75(298) *Journal of American Folklore* 283

Finlayson, Christopher and James Christmas, *He Kupu Taurangi: Treaty Settlements and the Future of Aotearoa New Zealand* (Huia, 2021)

Fischel, Daniel R, 'The Corporate Governance Movement' (1982) 35(6) *Vanderbilt Law Review* 1259

Fletcher, Ned, *The English Text of the Treaty of Waitangi* (Bridget Williams Books, 2022)

Fotios, Fitsilis, *Imposing Regulation on Advanced Algorithms* (Springer, 2019)

Freeman, Becky, Ross Mackenzie and Mike Daube, 'Should Tobacco and Alcohol Companies Be Allowed to Influence Australia's National Drug Strategy?' (2017) 27(2) *Public Health Research & Practice* <https://doaj.org/article/54c34fb9c3734550b54ed60f0e334a2a>

Friedman, Wolfgang, *Law in a Changing Society* (2nd ed, Penguin Books, 1972)

Fuller, Lon L, *The Morality of Law* (rev ed, Yale University Press, 1969)

Glaser, Daryl, 'South Africa and the Limits of Civil Society' (1997) 23(1) *Journal of Southern African Studies* 5

Godwin, Andrew, Steve Kourabas and Ian Ramsay, 'Twin Peaks and Financial Regulation' (2016) 49(3) *International Lawyer* 273

Goldsmith, Jack and Tim Wu, *Who Controls the Internet?: Illusions of a Borderless World* (Oxford University Press, 2006)

Gordon, Colin, 'Governmental Rationality: An Introduction' in G Burchell, C Gordon and P Miller (eds), *The Foucault Effect: Studies in Governmentality: With Two Lectures and an Interview with Michel Foucault* (University of Chicago Press, 1991) 1

'Governance', *National Indigenous Australians Agency* (Report) <https://www.niaa.gov.au/sites/default/files/publications/catsi-act-governance-factsheet.pdf>

Grandy, Christopher, 'New Jersey Corporate Chartermongering, 1875–1929' (1989) 49(3) *Journal of Economic History* 677

Grayling, Anthony, 'Social Evils and Social Good' in David Utting (ed), *Contemporary Social Evils* (Policy Press for Joseph Rowntree Foundation, 2009) 103

'Guiding Principles on Business and Human Rights: Implementing the United Nations "Protect, Respect and Remedy" Framework', *Office of the High Commission for Human Reports* (Report, 2011) <https://www.ohchr.org/sites/default/files/documents/publications/guidingprinciplesbusinesshr_en.pdf>

Habermas, Jürgen, *Between Facts and Norms: Contributions to a Discourse Theory of Law and Democracy*, tr William Rehg (MIT Press, 1996)

Hacker, Philipp, 'Corporate Governance for Complex Cryptocurrencies? A Framework for Stability and Decision Making in Blockchain-Based Organizations' *SSRN* (2017) <www.papers.ssrn.com>

Hahlo, HH and Ellison Kahn, *The South African Legal System and Its Background* (Juta & Co, 1968)

Hamburger, Philip A, 'Natural Rights, Natural Law, and American Constitutions' (1993) 102 *Yale Law Journal* 907

Harari, Yuval N, *Sapiens: A Brief History of Humankind* (Vintage, 2014)

Hardin, G, 'The Tragedy of the Commons' (1968) 162(3859) *Science* 1243

Harkins III, Malcolm J, 'The Uneasy Relationship of *Hobby Lobby*, *Conestoga Wood*, the Affordable Care Act, and the Corporate Person: How a Historical Myth Continues to Bedevil the Legal System' (2014) 7(2) *Saint Louis University Journal of Health Law & Policy* 201

Hartmann, Thom, *Unequal Protection: How Corporations Became "People" – And How You Can Fight Back* (2nd ed, Berrett-Koehler Publishers, 2010)

Hassan, Samer and Primavera De Filippi, 'The Expansion of Algorithmic Governance: From Code is Law to Law is Code' (2017) 17 *Field Actions Science Reports* 88

Hayek, FA, *The Constitution of Liberty* (Routledge and Kegan Paul, 1976, first published 1960)

Hazlehurst, Kayleen M, *Legal Pluralism and the Colonial Legacy: Indigenous Experiences of Justice in Canada, Australia and New Zealand* (Avebury, 1995)

Helfer, Laurence R and Graeme W Austin, *Human Rights and Intellectual Property: Mapping the Global Interface* (Cambridge University Press, 2011)

Henning, JJ, 'Close Corporations without End. Two Remarkable Decades of Simply "thinking small first"' (2007) 32(1) *Journal for Juridical Science* 187

Ho, Virginia Harper, '"Enlightened Shareholder Value": Corporate Governance Beyond the Shareholder-Stakeholder Divide' (2010) 36(1) *Journal of Corporation Law* 59

Holmes, Oliver Wendell, 'The Path of the Law' (1897) 10 *Harvard Law Review* 457

'Honouring the Truth, Reconciling for the Future Summary of the Final Report of the Truth and Reconciliation Commission of Canada' (Report, 2015) <https://ehprnh2mwo3.exactdn.com/wp-content/uploads/2021/01/Executive_Summary_English_Web.pdf>

Hunt, Paul, 'Reflections on International Human Rights Law and Cultural Rights' in Margaret Wilson and Paul Hunt (eds), *Culture, Rights, and Cultural Rights: Perspectives from the South Pacific* (Huia, 2000) 25

Hura, Nadine Anne, 'The Prospect of Co-governance Sparks Deep, Irrational Fears' *The Spinoff* (20 February 2020) <https://thespinoff.co.nz/atea/20-02-2023/the-prospect-of-co-governance-sparks-deep-irrational-fears>

Huxley, Julian, *UNESCO: Its Purpose and Its Philosophy* (UNESCO, 1946)

Iannone, A Pablo, *Dictionary of World Philosophy* (Routledge, online ed, 2001)

Inside Policy for the Office of the Registrar of Indigenous Corporations, 'The Corporations (Aboriginal and Torres Strait Islander) Act Review Consultation Report' (6 October 2017)

International Science Council, *A Guide for Policy-makers: Evaluating Rapidly Developing Technologies Including AI, Large Language Models and Beyond* (Paris, 2024)

Ireland, Paddy, Ian Grigg-Spall and Dave Kelly, 'The Conceptual Foundations of Modern Company Law' (1987) 14(1) *British Journal of Law and Society* 149

Ireland, Paddy, 'Limited Liability, Shareholder Rights and the Problem of Corporate Irresponsibility' (2010) 34 *Cambridge Journal of Economics* 837

Irvin-Erickson, Douglas, *Raphael Lemkin and the Concept of Genocide* (University of Pennsylvania Press, 2017)

Jensen, Michael C and William H Meckling, 'Theory of the Firm: Managerial Behavior, Agency Costs and Ownership Structure' (1976) 3(4) *Journal of Financial Economics* 305

Johnson, David R and David G Post, 'Law and Borders – The Rise of Law in Cyberspace' (1996) 48(5) *Stanford Law Review* 1367

'Joint Committee on Human Rights Sixth Report' (UK Parliament, 2003)

Jones, John Avery, 'Tax Law: Rules or Principles?' (1996) 17(3) *Fiscal Studies* 63

Jorgensen, Miriam (ed), *Rebuilding Native Nations: Strategies for Governance and Development* (University of Arizona Press, 2007)

Kahn-Freund, Otto, 'Reflections on Company Law Reform' (1944) 7(1/2) *Modern Law Review* 54

Kamalnath, Akshaya, 'Indigenous Corporations: Lessons from Maori Business Forms' (2021) 46(3) *Alternative Law Journal* 232

Kant, Immanuel, *Groundwork of the Metaphysics of Morals*, tr MJ Gregor (Cambridge University Press, 2006)

Keay, Andrew, 'Tackling the Issue of the Corporate Objective: An Analysis of the United Kingdom's "Enlightened Shareholder Value Approach"' (2007) 29(4) *Sydney Law Review* 577

Keay, Andrew, 'Ascertaining the Corporate Objective: An Entity Maximisation and Sustainability Model' (2008) 71(5) *Modern Law Review* 663

Keay, Andrew, 'Shareholder Primacy in Corporate Law: Can it Survive? Should it Survive?' (2010) 7(3) *European Company and Financial Law Review* 369

Keay, Andrew, *The Corporate Objective* (Edward Elgar, 2011)

Kerstein, Samuel, 'Treating Persons as Means' in Edward N Zalta and Uri Nodelman (eds), *The Stanford Encyclopedia of Philosophy* (Winter 2023 ed) <https://plato.stanford.edu/archives/win2023/entries/persons-means/>

Kirby, Michael, 'Australian Corporations Law and Global Forces' (1997) 2(1) *Flinders Journal of Law Reform* 41

Kirkham, Richard and Elizabeth A O'Loughlin, 'Judicial Review and Ombuds: A Systematic Analysis' (2020) *Public Law* 680

Kohl, Uta, *Jurisdiction and the Internet: Regulatory Competence over Online Activity* (Cambridge University Press, 2007)

Kostakopoulou, Dora, 'Floating Sovereignty: Pathology or a Necessary Means of State Evolution?' (2002) 22(1) *Oxford Journal of Legal Studies* 135

Kraakman, Reinier, et al., *Anatomy of Corporate Law* (Oxford University Press, 2004)

Kulick, Andreas, 'Corporate Human Rights?' (2021) 32(2) *European Journal of International Law* 537

Lash, Kurt T, *The Fourteenth Amendment and the Privileges and Immunities of American Citizenship* (Cambridge University Press, 2014)

Latty, Elvin R, 'Pseudo-Foreign Corporations' (1955) 65(2) *Yale Law Journal* 137

Laws, John, 'Law and Democracy' (1995) *Public Law* 72

Legg, Catherine and Christopher Hookway, 'Pragmatism' in Edward N Zalta (ed), *The Stanford Encyclopedia of Philosophy* (Summer 2021 ed) <https://plato.stanford.edu/archives/sum2021/entries/pragmatism/>

'Legislation Guidelines' *Legislation Design and Advisory Committee* (Report, 2021) <https://www.lac.org.nz/assets/documents/LDAC-Legislation-Guidelines-2021-edition.pdf>

Lehmann, AG, *The European Heritage: An Outline of Western Culture* (Guild Publishing, 1984)

Leigh, Andrew, 'The Rise and Fall of the Third Way' (Mar–Apr 2003) 75(2) *Australian Quarterly* 10

Lesaffer, Randall, 'Argument from Roman Law in Current International Law: Occupation and Acquisitive Prescription' (2005) 16(1) *European Journal of International Law* 25

Lessig, Lawrence, *Code Version 2.0* (Basic Books, 2006)

Levi-Faur, David, 'Regulatory Capitalism' in Peter Drahos (ed), *Regulatory Theory: Foundations and Applications* (ANU Press, 2017)

Ligon, Mellie, 'The Sovereign Citizen Movement: A Comparative Analysis with Similar Foreign Movements and Takeaways for the United States Judicial System' (2021) 35(2) *Emory International Law Review* 297

LoPucki, Lynn M, 'Algorithmic Entities' (2018) 95 *Washington University Law Review* 887

Loucaides, Loukis, *The European Convention on Human Rights: Collected Essays* (Brill, 2007)

Luhmann, Niklas, *Law as a Social System*, tr A Ziegert (Oxford University Press, 2004)

Lustig, Doreen and JHH Weiler, 'Judicial Review in the Contemporary World – Retrospective and Prospective' (2018) 16(2) *International Journal of Constitutional Law* 315

Machen Jr, Arthur W, 'Corporate Personality' (1910–11) 24(4) *Harvard Law Review* 253

MacIntyre, Alasdair, *After Virtue: A Study in Moral Theory* (3rd ed, Duckworth, 2007)

Macknight, CC, *The Voyage to Marege': Macassan Trepangers in Northern Australia* (Melbourne University Press, 1976)

Macpherson, Elizabeth, 'Iwi Companies' in Susan Watson and Lynne Taylor (eds), *Corporate Law in New Zealand* (Thomson Reuters, 2018) 111

Mandelbrot, Benoit B, *Fractals: Form, Chance, and Dimension* (WH Freeman, 1977)

Marique, Yseult, 'The Rule of Law and Administrative Justice' in Marc Hertog (ed), *The Oxford Handbook of Administrative Justice* (Oxford University Press, 2021) 305

Markus, Andrew, 'Genocide in Australia' (2001) 25 *Aboriginal History* 57

Merry, Sally Engle, 'Legal Pluralism' (1988) 22(5) *Law & Society Review* 869

McCrow-Young, Ally, 'Visibility, Power and Citizen Intervention the Five Eyes and New Zealand's Southern Cross Cable' (2017) 12(3) *Westminster Papers in Communication and Culture* 37

McKinnon, Malcolm, 'Colonial and Provincial Government' *Te Ara – the Encyclopedia of New Zealand* (Web Page, 6 October 2024) <https://teara.govt.nz/en/1966/maori-social-structure>

McLean, Janet, 'Legislative Invalidation, Human Rights Protection and s 4 of the New Bill of Rights Act' (2001) 4 *New Zealand Law Review* 421

Mercier, Ocean Ripeka, 'What Is Decolonisation?' in Bianca Elkington et al., *Imagining Decolonisation* (Bridget Williams Books, 2020) 40

Methven O'Brien, Claire and Roberto Caranta, *Due Diligence in EU Institutions' Own-Account Procurement: Rules and Practices* (Policy Department for Budgetary Affairs, European Parliament 2024)

Metzger, Michael B and Dan R Dalton, 'Seeing the Elephant: An Organizational Perspective on Corporate Moral Agency' (1996) 33(4) *American Business Law Journal* 489

Micheler, Eva, *Company Law: A Real Entity Theory* (Oxford University Press, 2017)

Mihalicz, Michael, *Indigenous Entrepreneurship* (Pressbooks, 2022)

Mik, Eliza, 'Private Lawmaking in Commercial Cyberspace' (2016) 23 *Pandora's Box* 115

Mikaere, Ani, *Colonising Myths Māori Realities He Rukuruku Whakaaro* (Huia, 2011)

Millard, Christopher, 'Blockchain and Law: Incompatible Codes?' (2018) 34 *Computer Law and Security Review* 843

Minow, Martha, *Applying Rights Rhetoric to Economic and Social Claims. Economic and Social Rights and the Right to Health* (Harvard University Press, 1995)

Mitchell, Lawrence E, *Progressive Corporate Law* (Routledge, 1996)

Moon, William J, 'Delaware's Global Competitiveness' (2021) 106(4) *Iowa Law Review* 1683

Morgan, Bronwen and Karen Yeung, *An Introduction to Law and Regulation: Text and Materials* (Cambridge University Press, 2007)

Morley, John, 'The Common Law Corporation: The Power of the Trust in Anglo-American Business History' (2016) 116(8) *Columbia Law Review* 2145

Morris, Christine, 'Indigenous Intellectual Property Rights: The Responsibilities of Maintaining the Oldest Continuous Culture in the World' (1997) 4(2) *Indigenous Law Bulletin* 9

Morsink, Johannes, *The Universal Declaration of Human Rights: Origins, Drafting, and Intent* (University of Pennsylvania Press, 1999)

Moses, Lyria Bennett, 'Adapting the Law to Technological Change: A Comparison of Common Law and Legislation' (2003) 26(3) *University of New South Wales Law Journal* 394

Mu, Honglei and Youngchan Lee, 'Greenwashing in Corporate Social Responsibility: A Dual-Faceted Analysis of Its Impact on Employee Trust and Identification' (2023) 15(22) *Sustainability* 15693

Mulgan, Geoff, *Connexity: How to Live in a Connected World* (Chatto & Windus, 1997)

Mulhall, Stephen and Andrew Swift, *Liberals and Communitarians* (Blackwell, 1995)

Murphy, Liam and Thomas Nagel, *The Myth of Ownership: Taxes and Justice* (Oxford University Press, 2005)

Narayanan, Arvind et al., *Bitcoin and Cryptocurrency Technologies: A Comprehensive Introduction* (Princeton University Press, 2016)

'Native Title Report 2007' (Aboriginal and Torres Strait Islander Social Justice Commissioner, 2007)

Neck, R, 'Neoclassical Economics: Origins, Evolution, and Critique' in D McCallum (ed), *The Palgrave Handbook of the History of Human Sciences* (Palgrave Macmillan, 2022)

Nehme, Marina, 'A Comparison of the Internal Governance Rules of Indigenous Corporations: Before and After the Introduction of the Corporations (Aboriginal and Torres Strait Islander) Act 2006' (2014) 29(1) *Australian Journal of Corporate Law* 71

Nehme, Marina, 'Indigenous Corporations and Accountability – the Evolution of the Directors' Duties' (2021) 36(3) *Australian Journal of Corporate Law* 240

Nehme, Marina, 'Aboriginal and Torres Strait Islander Corporations: Time for a Rethink?' (2023) 48(2) *Alternative Law Journal* 127

Nehme, Marina and John Francis Juriansz, 'The Evolution of Indigenous Corporations: Where to Now?' (2012) 33(1) *Adelaide Law Review* 101

Ngāi Tahu 2023 Annual Report (2023)

Nonet, Philippe, 'Legal Competence' in CM Campbell and Paul Wiles (eds), *Law and Society* (Martin Robertson, 1979) 268

Norman, Richard, *On Humanism* (Routledge, 2004)

Nussbaum, Martha, 'Women and Equality: The Capabilities Approach' (1999) 138(3) *International Labour Review* 227

Nygh, Peter, *Autonomy in International Contracts* (Oxford University Press, 1999)

Oxford English Dictionary (online)

Padfield, Stefan J, 'The Silent Role of Corporate Theory in the Supreme Court's Campaign Finance Cases' (2013) 15(3) *University of Pennsylvania Journal of Constitutional Law* 831

Padfield, Stefan J, 'Rehabilitating Concession Theory' (2014) 66 *Oklahoma Law Review* 327

Palmer, EE, 'Directors' Powers and Duties' in Jacob S Ziegel (ed), *Canadian Company Law* (Butterworths, 1967)

Pettit, Philip, 'Minority Claims under Two Conceptions of Democracy' in Duncan Ivison, Paul Patton and Will Sanders (eds), *Political Theory and the Rights of Indigenous Peoples* (Cambridge University Press, 2000) 199

Phillips, Michael J, 'Reappraising the Real Entity Theory of the Corporation' (1994) 21 *Florida State University Law Review* 1061

Porterfield, Amanda, *Corporate Spirit: Religion and the Rise of the Modern Corporation* (Oxford University Press, 2018)

Powell, Thomas Reed, 'The Changing Law of Foreign Corporations' (1918) 33(4) *Political Science Quarterly* 549

'Principles Respecting the Government of Canada's Relationship with Indigenous Peoples', *Department of Justice Canada* (Report, 2018) <https://www.rcaanc-cirnac.gc.ca/eng/1379594359150/1607905375821>

Qu, Hong, 'The Ends of Artificial Intelligence' in Seth Rudy and Rachel Scarborough King (eds), *The Ends of Knowledge* (Bloomsbury Academic, 2023) 139

Rand, Ayn, *Virtue of Selfishness: A New Concept of Egoism* (Centennial, 1964)

Rao, Neomi, 'Three Concepts of Dignity in Constitutional Law' (2013) 86(1) *Notre Dame Law Review* 183

'Recognition of the Legal Personality of Foreign Commercial Corporations' (1928) 22(1) *American Journal of International Law* 157

Retry, Stefan, 'Mandatory Worker Representation on the Board and Its Effect on Shareholder Wealth' (2018) 47(1) *Financial Management* 25

Rhee, Robert J, 'A Legal Theory of Shareholder Primacy' (2018) 102 *Minnesota Law Review* 1951

Rishworth, Paul et al., *The New Zealand Bill of Rights* (Oxford University Press, 2003)

Romano, Roberta, 'After the Revolution in Corporate Law' (2005) 55(3) *Journal of Legal Education* 342

Ross, Mike, 'The Throat of Parata' in Bianca Elkington et al., *Imagining Decolonisation* (Bridget Williams Books, 2020) 21

'Royal Commission into the Robodebt Scheme Report Volume 1' (Commonwealth of Australia, 2023)

'Royal Proclamation 1763: Relationships, Rights and Treaties' *Government of Canada* (Report, 2013) <www.rcaanc-cirnac.gc.ca/eng/1379594359150/1607905375821>

Runciman, David, *The Handover: How We Gave Control of Our Lives to Corporations, States and AIs* (Profile Books, 2023)

Russell, Bertrand, *History of Western Philosophy and Its Connection with Political and Social Circumstances from the Earliest Times to the Present* (2nd ed, Routledge, 1961)

Salter, Alexander William, *The Political Economy of Distributism: Property, Liberty, and the Common Good* (Catholic University of America Press, 2023)

Savic, Katarina and Christina E Hoicka, 'Indigenous Legal Forms and Governance Structures in Renewable Energy: Assessing the Role and Perspectives of First Nations Economic Development Corporations' (2023) 101 *Energy Research & Social Science* 10321, 1

Scherer, Matthew U, 'Of Wild Beasts and Digital Analogs: The Legal Status of Autonomous Systems' (2018) 19(1) *Nevada Law Journal* 259

Schulz, Armin W, 'Tools of the Trade: The Bio-cultural Evolution of the Human Propensity to Trade' (2022) 37(8) *Biology & Philosophy* <https://doi.org/10.1007/s10539-022-09837-2>

Shiva, Vandana, *Water Wars: Privatization, Pollution and Profit* (Southend Press, 2002)

Slattery, Brian, 'The Hidden Constitution: Aboriginal Rights in Canada' (1984) 32(2) *American Journal of Comparative Law* 361

Smith, Linda Tuhiwai, *Decolonizing Methodologies: Research and Indigenous Peoples* (2nd ed, Zed Books, 2012)

Solomon, Lewis D, 'On the Frontier of Capitalism: Implementation of Humanomics by Modern Publicly Held Corporations: A Critical Assessment' (1993) 50(4) *Washington and Lee Law Review* 1625

Srnicek, Nick, 'The Challenges of Platform Capitalism: Understanding the Logic of a New Business Model' (2017) 23(4) *Juncture* 254

Stacey, Richard, 'Proportionality Analysis by the South African Constitutional Court' in Mordechai Kremnitzer, Talya Steiner and Andrej Lang (eds), *Proportionality in Action: Comparative and Empirical Perspectives on the Judicial Practice* (Cambridge University Press, 2020) 193

Stolzenberg, Nomi, 'The Culture of Property' in R Schweder, M Minow and H Markus (eds), *Engaging with Cultural Differences: The Multicultural Challenge in Liberal Democracies* (Sage Foundation, 2002) 177

Stone, Damian, 'Maori Economic Development and Asset Utilisation' (2006) 1 *New Zealand Law Journal* 30

Sunstein, Cass R, *Valuing Life: Humanizing the Regulatory State* (University of Chicago Press, 2014)

Sunstein, Cass R and Adrian Vermeule, 'The Morality of Administrative Law' (2018) 131(7) *Harvard Law Review* 1924

Swanson, Gillian, 'Collectivity, Human Fulfilment and the "Force of Life": Wilfred Trotter's Concept of the Herd Instinct in Early 20th-Century Britain' (2014) 27(1) *History of the Human Sciences* 21

Taylor, James, 'Criminalising Fraud: Victorian Responses to Company Scandals' (2011) 32(10) *Company Lawyer* 291

Taylor, Lynn, 'Corporate Enterprises' in Susan Watson and Lynn Taylor (eds), *Corporate Law in New Zealand* (Thomson Reuters, 2018) 97

Te Aho, Linda, 'Corporate Governance: Balancing Tikanga Maori with Commercial Objectives' (2005) 8(2) *Yearbook of New Zealand Jurisprudence* 300

Thaler, Richard H and Cass R Sunstein, *Nudge: Improving Decisions About Health, Wealth And Happiness* (Penguin Books, 2009)

The Independent Working Group on Constitutional Transformation, 'He Whakaaro Here Whakaumu Mō Aotearoa: The Report of Matike Mai Aotearoa' (2016) 49

Tierney, Brian, *Foundations of the Conciliar Theory: The Contribution of the Medieval Canonists from Gratian to the Great Schism* (Brill, 1997)

Toope, Stephen, 'Cultural Diversity and Human Rights' (1997) 42 *McGill Law Journal* 169

'Traditional Social Structure' in A McLintock (ed), *An Encyclopaedia of New Zealand* (Web Page, 1966) <https://teara.govt.nz/en/1966/maori-social-structure>

'Truth and Reconciliation Commission of Canada' *Government of Canada* (Web Page, 2022) <https://www.rcaanc-cirnac.gc.ca/eng/1450124405592/1529106060525#chp1>

Tse, Nathan, 'Decentralised Autonomous Organisations and the Corporate Form' (2020) 51(2) *Victoria University of Wellington Law Review* 313

Turner, Fred, *From Counterculture to Cyberculture: Stewart Brand, the Whole Earth Network, and the Rise of Digital Utopianism* (University of Chicago Press, 2006)

UN AI Advisory Board, 'Interim Report: Governing AI for Humanity' (Report, 2023) <https://www.un.org/sites/un2.un.org/files/ai_advisory_body_interim_report.pdf>

Vining, Aidan R and John Richards, 'Indigenous Economic Development in Canada: Confronting Principal-agent and Principal–principal Problems to Reduce Resource Rent Dissipation' (2016) 49 *Resources Policy* 358

'Waka Umanga: A Proposed Law for Māori Governance Entities' (NZLC R92, 2006)

'Waka Umanga (Māori Corporations) Bill Commentary' *New Zealand Legislation* (Report, 2007)

Wallerstein, Immanuel, 'Braudel on Capitalism, or Everything Upside Down' (1991) 63(2) *Journal of Modern History* 354

Watson, Susan, 'The Corporate Legal Entity as a Fund' (2018) 6 *Journal of Business Law* 467

Watson, Susan, *The Making of the Modern Company* (Hart Publishing, 2022)

Williams, Richard, 'Enlightened Shareholder Value in UK Company Law' (2012) 35(1) *UNSW Law Journal* 360

Winner, Langdon, 'Do Artifacts Have Politics?' (1980) 109(1) *Daedalus* 121

Worthington, Michelle and Peta Spender, 'Constructing Legal Personhood: Corporate Law's Legacy' (2021) 30(3) *Griffith Law Review* 348

Young, Frankie, 'Indigenous Economic Development and Sustainability: Maintaining the Integrity of Indigenous Culture in Corporate Governance' (2021) 17(2) *McGill Journal of Sustainable Development Law* 149

Zetzsche, Dirk A, Ross P Buckley and Douglas W Arner, 'The Distributed Liability of Distributed Ledgers: Legal Risks of Blockchain' [2017] *University of New South Wales Research Study* 1

Cases

Australia

JT International SA v Commonwealth of Australia, British American Tobacco Australasia Limited v The Commonwealth [2012] HCA 43
Lange v Australian Broadcasting Corporation [1997] HCA 25
Mabo v Queensland (No 2) [1992] HCA 23
Wik Peoples v Queensland [1996] HCA 40

Canada

BCE v 1976 Debentureholders [2008] 3 SCR 560
Irwin Toy Ltd v Quebec (A-G) [1989] 1 SCR 927
R v Big M Drug Mart Ltd [1985] 1 SCR 295
RJR-MacDonald Inc v Attorney General of Canada [1995] 3 SCR 199
Yahey v British Columbia 2021 BCSC 1287

European Court of Human Rights

OAO Neftyanaya Kompaniya Yukos v Russia, application no 14902/04, judgment dated 31 July 2014
Société Colas Est v France, application no. 37971/97, judgment dated 16 April 2002
Sunday Times v United Kingdom, application no 6538/74, judgment dated 26 April 1979

New Zealand

Chirnside v Fay [2007] NZSC 68
Meridian Global Funds Management Asia Ltd v Securities Commission [1995] 3 NZLR 7 (PC)
New Zealand Air Line Pilots' Association Inc v Attorney-General [1997] 3 NZLR 269
Trans-Tasman Resources Limited v Taranaki-Whanganui Conservation Board [2021] NZSC 127
Westco Lagan Ltd v Attorney-General [2001] 1 NZLR 40
Wiseline Corporation Ltd, Re (2002) 16 PRNZ 347 (CA)

South Africa

First National Bank of South Africa v Commissioner, SARS [2002] ZACC 5
Government of the Republic of South Africa v Grootboom [2000] ZACC 19

Investigating Directorate: SEO v Hyundai Motor Distributors (Pty) Ltd [2000] ZACC 12
Minister of Health v Treatment Action Campaign [2002] ZACC 15
Soobramoney v Minister of Health (Kwazulu-Natal) [1997] ZACC 17

United Kingdom

Cardiff Savings Bank, Re [1892] 2 Ch 100 (Marquess of Bute's case)
Daimler Co Ltd v Continental Tyre and Rubber Co (Great Britain) Ltd [1916] UKHL 845
HL Bolton (Engineering) Co Ltd v TJ Graham & Sons Ltd [1957] 1 QB 159
Prest v Petrodel Resources Limited [2013] UKSC 34
R (Factortame Ltd) v Secretary of State for Transport [1991] UKHL 7
Rolloswin Investments Ltd v Chromolit Portugal Cutelarias e Produtos Metálicos SARL [1970] 2 All ER 673
Salomon v A Salomon & Co Ltd [1896] UKHL 1

United States

Bank of Augusta v Earle 38 US 519 (1839)
Burwell v Hobby Lobby Stores, Inc 573 US 682 (2014)
Citizens United v Federal Election Commission 558 US 310 (2010)
Dartmouth College v Woodward 17 US 518 (1819)
McGirt v Oklahoma 591 US ___ (2020)
Santa Clara County v Southern Pacific Railroad Company 118 US 394 (1886)

Legislation

Australia

Administrative Decisions (Judicial Review) Act 1977
Australian Human Rights Commission Act 1986
Charter of Human Rights and Responsibilities Act 2006 (Vic)
Commonwealth Electoral Act 1918
Commonwealth Electoral Act 1962
Commonwealth of Australia Constitution Act 1900
Corporations Act 2001
Corporations (Aboriginal and Torres Strait Islander) Act 2006
Human Rights Act 2004 (ACT)
Native Title Act 1993
Noongar (Koorah, Nitja, Boordahwan) (Past, Present, Future) Recognition Act 2016 (WA)
Taxation Administration Act 1953

British Virgin Islands

BVI Business Companies Act 2004

Canada

Business Corporations Act [SNWT (Nu) 1996] c 19
Constitution Acts 1867
Constitution Act 1982
Declaration on the Rights of Indigenous Peoples Act [SBC 2019] c 44
First Nations Commercial and Industrial Development Act [SC 2005] c 53
Indian Act 1876
United Nations Declaration on the Rights of Indigenous Peoples Act [SC 2021] c 14

European Union

European Union (Preventive Restructuring) Regulations 2022
EU Artificial Intelligence Act, 2023

Ireland

Constitution of Ireland 1937
Companies Act 2014
European Union (Preventive Restructuring) Regulations 2022 SI No 380 of 2022

New Zealand

Charitable Trusts Act 1957
Charities Act 2005
Companies Act 1993
Companies Amendment Act 2014
Copyright Act 1994
Income Tax Act 2007
Limited Partnerships Act 2008
New Zealand Bill of Rights Act 1990
Partnership Law Act 2019
Regulatory Systems (Commercial Matters) Amendment Act 2017
Te Ture Whenua Māori Act 1993
Trade Marks Act 2002
Treaty of Waitangi Act 1975

South Africa

Close Corporations Act 1984
Companies Act 2008
Constitution of the Republic of South Africa 1996
Promotion of Administrative Justice Act 2000

United Kingdom

Companies Act 1862
Joint Stock Companies Act 1844
Limited Liability Act 1855
Magna Carta 1215, 1297

United States

Arizona Revised Statutes 44-7003 (2017)
'Executive Order on the Safe, Secure, and Trustworthy Development and Use of Artificial Intelligence' (President of the United States, 30 October 2023)
Patient Protection and Affordable Health Care Act of 2010
Religious Freedom Restoration Act of 1993

International instruments

European Convention for the Protection of Human Rights and Fundamental Freedoms ETS 5 (3 September 1950)
Inter-American Commission on Human Rights (IACHR), *American Declaration of the Rights and Duties of Man*, 2 May 1948
Mi'kmaq Peace and Friendship Treaty, signed 15 December 1725 (entered into force 4 June 1726)
Protect, Respect and Remedy: a Framework for Business and Human Rights: Report of the Special Representative of the Secretary-General on the Issue of Human Rights and Transnational Corporations and Other Business Enterprises, A/HRC/8/5, UN Human Rights Council, 7 April 2008
Protocol 1 to the *European Convention for the Protection of Human Rights and Fundamental Freedoms* ETS 9 (20 March 1952)
The World Conference on Human Rights, *Vienna Declaration and Programme of Action,* A/CONF.157/23, UN General Assembly, 12 July 1993
Treaty of Waitangi/Te Tiriti o Waitangi 1840
UN General Assembly, *Universal Declaration of Human Rights*, GA Res 217A (III), UN GAOR, UN Doc A/810 (10 December 1948)
UN General Assembly, *International Convention on the Elimination of All Forms of Racial Discrimination*, UNTS, vol 660, p 195, 21 December 1965
UN General Assembly, *International Covenant on Economic, Social and Cultural Rights*, UNTS, vol 993, p 3, 16 December 1966
UN General Assembly, *International Covenant on Civil and Political Rights*, UNTS, vol 999, p 171, 16 December 1966
UN General Assembly, *Convention on the Elimination of All Forms of Discrimination Against Women*, UNTS, vol 1249, p 13, 18 December 1979
UN General Assembly, *Convention Against Torture and Other Cruel, Inhuman or Degrading Treatment or Punishment*, UNTS vol 1465, p 85, 10 December 1984
UN General Assembly, *Convention on the Rights of the Child*, UNTS, vol 1577, p 3, 20 November 1989

UN General Assembly, *Convention on the Rights of Persons with Disabilities: Resolution / Adopted by the General Assembly*, A/RES/61/106, 24 January 2007

UN General Assembly, *United Nations Declaration on the Rights of Indigenous Peoples: Resolution/Adopted by the General Assembly*, A/RES/61/295, 2 October 2007

Other

'About B Corp Certification', *B Lab* (Web Page, 2024) <https://www.bcorporation.net/en-us/certification/>

'About us', *Office of the Registrar of Indigenous Corporations* (Web Page) <https://www.oric.gov.au/about-us>

'Action 2 Neutralising the Effects of Hybrid Mismatch Arrangements', *OECD* (Web Page) <https://www.oecd.org/tax/beps/beps-actions/action2/>

'Amsterdam Declaration', *Humanists International* (Web Page) <https://humanists.international/what-is-humanism/the-amsterdam-declaration>

'Annual Report Statistics', *Delaware Division of Corporations* (Web Page) <https://corp.delaware.gov/stats/>

Barlow, John Perry, 'A Declaration of the Independence of Cyberspace', *Electronic Frontier Foundation* (Web Page, 1996) <https://www.eff.org/cyberspace-independence>

'BEPS Actions', *OECD* (Web Page) <https://www.oecd.org/tax/beps/beps-actions/>

Bilton, Nick, 'Silicon Valley's Most Disturbing Obsession', *Vanity Fair* (online, 5 November 2016) <https://www.vanityfair.com/news/2016/10/silicon-valley-ayn-rand-obsession>

'Britain Needs Business at its Best', *Better Business Act* (Web Page, 2024) <https://betterbusinessact.org/>

British American Tobacco New Zealand, 'Proposal to Introduce Plain Packaging of Tobacco Products in New Zealand: Submission by British American Tobacco (New Zealand) Limited', *AgreeDisagree.co.nz* (2013)

'BVI Company Incorporation And Partnership Formation', *Ogier* (Web Page, 17 January 2019) <https://www.ogier.com/publications/bvi-company-incorporation-and-partnership-formation>

Cassim, Rehana, 'Piercing the Corporate Veil "Unconscionable abuse" under the Companies Act 71 of 2008', *De Rebus* (online, 1 August 2012) <https://www.derebus.org.za/piercing-corporate-veil-unconscionable-abuse-companies-act-71-2008/>

Cenziper, Debbie and Will Fitzgibbon, 'The 'Cowboy Cocktail': How Wyoming Became One of the World's Top Tax Havens', *The Washington Post* (online, 20 December 2021) <https://www.washingtonpost.com/business/interactive/2021/wyoming-trusts-finance-pandora-papers/>

'Close Corporations (CC)', *SARS* (2021) <https://www.sars.gov.za>

'Companies Register', *New Zealand Companies Office* (Web Page, 2022) <https://companies-register.companiesoffice.govt.nz/>

'Conventions and Recommendations', *International Labour Organisation* (Web Page, 1996–2004) <https://www.ilo.org>

Economy, Elizabeth C, 'The Great Firewall of China: Xi Jinping's Internet Shutdown', *The Guardian* (online, 29 June 2018) <https://www.theguardian.com/news/2018/jun/29/the-great-firewall-of-china-xi-jinpings-internet-shutdown>

Emamian, Milad, 'The Cowboy State Tames Bitcoin's Regulatory Wild West', *The Regulatory Review* (Web Page, 7 April 2021) <https://www.theregreview.org/2021/04/07/emamian-cowboy-state-tames-bitcoins-regulatory-wild-west/>

'EU AI Act: First Regulation on Artificial Intelligence', *European Parliament* (Web Page, 2023) <https://www.europarl.europa.eu/topics/en/article/20230601STO93804/eu-ai-act-first-regulation-on-artificial-intelligence>

Evans, Rachel, 'What if whales Took Us to Court? A Move to Grant them Legal Personhood Would Include the Right to Sue', *The Conversation* (Web Page, 15 April 2024) <https://theconversation.com/what-if-whales-took-us-to-court-a-move-to-grant-them-legal-personhood-would-include-the-right-to-sue-227335>

Falkon, Samuel, 'The Story of the DAO – Its History and Consequences', *Medium* (Web Page, 25 December 2017) <https://medium.com/swlh/the-story-of-the-dao-its-history-and-consequences-71e6a8a551ee>

'First Nations Commercial and Industrial Development Act', *Government of Canada* (Web Page, 2023) <https://www.sac-isc.gc.ca/eng/1100100033561/1612128155378>

Friedman, Milton, 'The Social Responsibility of Business Is to Increase Its Profits', *The New York Times* (New York, 13 September 1970) SM 17

Ganado, Max, 'Legal Personality For Blockchains, DAOs and Smart Contracts', *Mondaq Business Briefing* (Web Page, 6 June 2018) <https://www.mondaq.com/fin-tech/707696/legal-personality-for-blockchains-daos-and-smart-contracts>

Gleason, Patrick, 'Regulatory Sandboxes Give States An Edge Attracting Innovation and Investment', *Forbes* (online, 21 December 2021) <https://www.forbes.com/sites/patrickgleason/2021/12/31/regulatory-sandboxes-give-states-an-edge-attracting-innovation-and-investment/?sh=1d130cd97003>

'Hardly Child's Play: North Carolina Joins the Growing Number of States With a FinTech Regulatory Sandbox', *The National Law Review* (Web Page, 19 October 2021) <https://www.natlawreview.com/article/hardly-child-s-play-north-carolina-joins-growing-number-states-fintech-regulatory>

Hoicka, Christina E and Matthew Foss, 'How Indigenous Economic Development Corporations can Support a Just, Low-carbon Energy Transition', *The Conversation* (Web Page, 27 June 2023) <https://theconversation.com/how-indigenous-economic-development-corporations-can-support-a-just-low-carbon-energy-transition-206976>

'How the Blockchain Can Transform Government', *Knowledge@Wharton* (Web Page, 5 July 2018) <www.knowledge.wharton.upenn.edu/article/blockchain-can-transform-government/>

'Indigenous People and Nature: A Tradition of Conservation', *UN Environmental Programme* (Web Page, 26 April 2017) <https://www.unep.org/news-and-stories/story/indigenous-people-and-nature-tradition-conservation>

'Information & Guidance', *CEA* (Web Page, 2024) <https://cea.gov.ie/en-ie/Publications/Information-Guidance>

'International Regulatory Co-operation – Transforming Rulemaking to Meet the Global Challenges of the 21st Century', *OECD* (Web Page) <https://www.oecd.org/gov/regulatory-policy/irc.htm>

'Inuit Business and Federal Procurement', *Government of Canada* (Web Page, 2022) <https://www.sac-isc.gc.ca/eng/1646147382130/1648487162865>

'IWGIA', International Work Group for Indigenous Affairs (Web Page) <www.iwgia.org>

Johnson, David R and David G Post, 'The Great Debate – Law in the Virtual World' (2006) 11(2) *First Monday* <https://doi.org/10.5210/fm.v11i2.1311>

Krugman, Paul, 'A.I. May Change Everything, but Probably Not Too Quickly', *The New York Times* (online, 31 March 2023) <https://www.nytimes.com/2023/03/31/opinion/ai-chatgpt-jobs-economy.html>

'Leaky Building Syndrome – NZ, Canada and Australian Experiences', *Lovegrove & Cotton* (Web Page, 26 September 2022) <https://lclawyers.com.au/leaky-building-syndrome-nz-canada-and-australian-experiences/>

Macheel, Tanaya, 'The DAO Might Be Groundbreaking, But Is It Legal?', *American Banker* (Web Page, 20 May 2016) <https://www.americanbanker.com/news/the-dao-might-be-groundbreaking-but-is-it-legal>

Manjoo, Farhad, 'What BlackRock, Vanguard and State Street Are Doing to the Economy', *The New York Times* (online, 12 May 2022) <https://www.nytimes.com/2022/05/12/opinion/vanguard-power-blackrock-state-street.html>

'Māori Population Estimates: Mean Year Ended 31 December 2023 (2018-base)', *Stats NZ* (Web Page, 16 May 2024) <https://www.stats.govt.nz/information-releases/maori-population-estimates-mean-year-ended-31-december-2023/>

Marantz, Andrew, 'O.K., Doomer', *The New Yorker* (New York, 18 March 2024) 42

Morozov, Evgeny, 'Two Decades of the Web: A Utopia no Longer', *Prospect* (online, 22 June 2011) <https://www.prospectmagazine.co.uk/ideas/technology/49273/two-decades-of-the-web-a-utopia-no-longer>

Ng, Kenneth, 'Finding DAOism', *Medium* (Web Page, 29 June 2016) <https://medium.com/blockchainedu/finding-daoism-683246830c90>

Nippert, Matt, 'Shell Company Barriers in Place', *Sunday-Star Times* (online, 29 June 2014) <https://www.pressreader.com/new-zealand/sunday-star-times/20140629/282329678033251>

'Nunavut, Canada's Third Territory North of 60', *Government of Canada* (Web Page, 2024) <https://www.rcaanc-cirnac.gc.ca/eng/1303138100962/1536244277979>

'Our Participants', *United Nations Global Compact* (Web Page, 2024) <https://unglobalcompact.org/what-is-gc/participants>

Patel, Deep, '8 Ways Generation Z Will Differ From Millennials In The Workplace', *Forbes* (online, 21 September 2017) <https://www.forbes.com/sites/deeppatel/2017/09/21/8-ways-generation-z-will-differ-from-millennials-in-the-workplace/?sh=2e6e8d7e76e5>

'Pedagogy, Andragogy, & Heutagogy', *Center for Online Learning, Research and Service, University of Illinois Springfield* (Web Page, 2022) <https://www.uis.edu>

Popper, Nathaniel, 'A Venture Fund with Plenty of Virtual Capital, but No Capitalist', *The New York Times* (online, 22 May 2016) <https://www.nytimes.com/2016/05/22/business/dealbook/crypto-ether-bitcoin-currency.html>

Popper, Nathaniel, 'Paper Points Up Flaws in Venture Fund Based on Virtual Money', *The New York Times* (online, 27 May 2016) <https://www.nytimes.com/2016/05/28/business/dealbook/paper-points-up-flaws-in-venture-fund-based-on-virtual-money.html>

Rademaker, Laura, Jakelin Troy and Jakelin Troy, 'Friday Essay: 'Too many Aboriginal Babies' – Australia's Secret History of Aboriginal Population Control in the 1960s', *The Conversation* (Web Page, 12 April 2024) <https://theconversation.com/friday-essay-too-many-aboriginal-babies-australias-secret-history-of-aboriginal-population-control-in-the-1960s-189249>

'Regulatory Policy by Country', *OECD* <https://www.oecd.org/gov/regulatory-policy/by-country.htm>

'Responsible Investment', *Norges Bank Investment Management* (Web Page) <https://www.nbim.no/en/responsible-investment/>

'Small Business', *Ministry of Business, Innovation and Employment* (Web Page, 2024) <www.mbie.govt.nz>

Smith, Bryan, 'The Story of the DAO, and How it Shaped Ethereum', *Coin Insider* (Web Page, 23 May 2018) <www.coininsider.com>

Stock, Rob, 'The "Rottenomics" of the $47 billion Leaky Homes Market Failure' *Stuff* (Web Page, 3 October 2019) <https://www.stuff.co.nz/business/116236850/the-rottenomics-of-the-47-billion-leaky-homes-market-failure>

Thomas, David, 'Is South African Transformation Dead?', *African Business* (Web Page, 1 September 2020) <https://african.business/2020/09/economy/black-economic-power-matters-is-south-african-transformation-dead>

Toobin, Jeffrey, 'After Kennedy', *The New Yorker* (New York, 9 July 2018) 19

'Universal Declaration of Human Rights', *United Nations* (Web Page) <https://www.un.org>

Weiser, Martin, 'North Korea: Law, but not as We Know It', *theinterpreter* (Web Page, 25 November 2021) <https://www.lowyinstitute.org/the-interpreter/north-korea-law-not-we-know-it>

Wellauer, Kirstie, Carly Williams and Bridget Brennan, 'Why the Voice Failed', *ABC* (Web Page, 16 October 2023) <https://www.abc.net.au/news/2023-10-16/why-the-voice-failed/102978962>

'Why Intellectual Property is Essential for your Business', *World Intellectual Property Organization* (Web Page) <http//www.wipo.int/sme/en/>

WimlerHale, 'SEC Confirms Certain ICOs Are Securities Offerings; Regulators Renew Focus On Cryptocurrencies', *Mondaq* (Web Page, 7 August 2017) <www.wilmerhale.com>

World Intellectual Property Organization in Collaboration with the Office of the United Nations High Commissioner for Human Rights, *Intellectual Property and Human Rights* (Report, 1998) <https://www.wipo.int/edocs/pubdocs/en/wipo_pub_762.pdf>

Index

Page numbers in **bold reference tables

FSC
www.fsc.org
MIX
Papier | Fördert
gute Waldnutzung
FSC® C083411

Kolibri 360 GmbH
Ferdinand-Jühlke-Straße 7
99095 Erfurt, Deutschland
produktsicherheit@kolibri360.de